From BEING WHERE YOU ARE

- There is no such thing as the experience of freedom without design and control.

- I am not my body, my mind, my heart. I Am. What am I? What are you? You can look where you will, you can't find it. But you can be it.

- Shame is never a creative motivation.

- To be completely independent of God—that is death.

- Heaven and earth are one. Only man, in his foolishness, tries to separate them.

BEING WHERE YOU ARE

LORD MARTIN CECIL

The one who has heretofore been known as
Bishop Martin Cecil, or Lord Martin Cecil, is
now identified by his British title, Lord Exeter,
or (more formally) The Marquess of Exeter.

Keats Publishing, Inc.   New Canaan, Connecticut

BEING WHERE YOU ARE

Published by Keats Publishing, Inc.
212 Elm Street,
New Canaan, Connecticut 06840 U.S.A.

Library of Congress Catalog Card Number: 73-93652

International Standard Book Number: 0-87983-071-9

Printed in the United States of America

Contents

Page

Foreword 7

Introduction 9

The Cosmos and You 11

Potential Released 19

The Art of Peace in a World of War 29

God—The Creative Compulsion 45

The Snare of the Fowler 55

The Worth of Work 65

The Authority of Doing 77

Unashamed to Praise the Lord 91

No! 103

The Passing of Restrictions 114

The Salvation of God 129

What of the New Age? 140

Heaven and Earth Are One! 150

Your Significance 162

Be Thou Perfect 178

Return to Being 192

To Guide You 203

Foreword

All my life I have known there was more to living than what has been experienced by the vast numbers of people throughout the centuries. That search for "more" brought me to many different places and what I discovered can be summed up in a phrase found on a contemporary poster: "Bloom where you are planted" —BE who you really are where you are in the present moment.

To hear this proclaimed in word is one thing but to see it revealed constantly and consistently in everyday living, not only by one man but by an increasing number of men and women in groups all across the United States and Canada concerned with true identity and right expression, is quite another.

The quality of instruction and inspiration contained in these talks by Lord Martin Cecil has profoundly affected not only my own life and that of the members of my family but countless others: high school and college youth looking for an alternative to drugs, young adults desiring to experience meaningful interpersonal relationships, and people of all ages who have come to accept that the answer is not in some other time or some other place but is in Being who you are where you are.

I wholeheartedly and enthusiastically recommend to

all those with integrity a thoughtful reading of the good news found within the covers of this most significant book.

— George Franklin Emery, BSc (Ed), STB

Introduction

There are some who have high hopes that the genius of man will once more bring the human race successfully through this present time of proliferating crises. If the genius of man is considered to be the power of his intellect, then his hopes may well be vain. Is it not his mental prowess, combined with his emotional instability, under the motivation of the all-encompassing egocentricity of his attitude, that generates the crises?

However, if the genius of man is recognized as the transcendent quality of his true character, presently obscured by his humanitarian egocentricity, then there is indeed not only hope but certainty. The subject matter of this book speaks of the true genius of man. This reference to man only ceases to be a platitude when the reader accepts the word as referring to himself.

Some of the terms used in these transcribed talks are taken from the religious vocabulary, particularly that of Christianity. This is so because they were spoken to people gathered in a setting where such an approach was fitting. Other ways of saying the same thing could be used; no one needs to be hung up on words. These are merely symbols of a reality in any case. Let us share a mutual concern to discover the reality that is thus symbolized, through our own increasing experience of it. I trust that the following chapters may help.

— Martin Cecil
October 30, 1973

The Cosmos and You

Life has design and purpose, a design and purpose which are all-inclusive. Human beings have a certain scope of awareness. That scope of awareness has in recent decades been increasing, but no matter how much it may increase, the awareness capable of being encompassed by the human mind could only be the minutest fraction of all there is to be encompassed. Knowledge is a bottomless pit. The more involved the mind of man becomes with knowledge, the more opportunity there is to distort the design and purpose of life. If we should operate a vehicle that is capable of going only five miles an hour we can, perhaps, have a head-on collision with another vehicle going five miles per hour without too much damage. But if through the increase of knowledge we have vehicles which are going one hundred miles an hour and they meet head-on, obviously the trouble has increased. And so it is in every sphere of man's function. While he did not have too much knowledge he could not do too much damage, even though he functioned wrongly. However, continuing to function wrongly and increasing knowledge, problems are multiplied, damage is increased, disaster becomes inevitable.

Clearly, then, we may recognize the trouble that is being caused by man's wrong function. This trouble is limited in scope, insofar as the cosmic whole is concerned, but it looms large in the experience of human beings on earth. Man's wrong function is based in the fact that his own mind ignores life's design and purpose, substituting designs and purposes conceived by the mind itself. These designs and purposes have changed very little over the length of man's historical past, but the methods used to achieve the designs and purposes have become more sophisticated because of the constant increase of knowledge, the constant delving in the bottomless pit. If this continues to its ultimate conclusion, then obviously man, with his mind, is eliminated from the face of the earth.

However, if life has a design and a purpose, then obviously man would not be here if he was not included in that design and purpose. Concern, therefore, should be with the rediscovery and the experience of the real nature of life's design and purpose. Life's design and purpose already exist. The very fact that the cosmos exists, the very fact that we exist, reveals this. But as long as man's mind thinks to rule, there is only one end—for man; I doubt if he has the power to end the cosmos. Because life has a design and a purpose, there is indication of the reality of the being of One who may be called the Father. The Father, used in this sense, describes the overall ground of all being from whence springs the cosmic all-that-is. The cosmic all-that-is gives evidence of the reality of the Father. Words have to be used to describe what is in fact indescribable. The word "Father" can convey a picture, can initiate an awareness, of whatever the reality is to which the word refers. The cosmos as a whole, whatever it is—the human mind certainly doesn't know what it is—reveals the reality of the Father.

But there is something specific that should naturally come to point, even in this minute portion of the cosmic whole. Whatever it is that should be brought to point here in this little planet requires certain machinery to do it, to translate the cosmic whole into a specific expression of life's design and purpose here on earth. The design and purpose so revealed will not be unrelated, of course, to the rest of the cosmos. It is perhaps a miniature evidence of what is true of the rest of the cosmos, translated into the particular terms that are possible here on earth. What is possible here on earth is determined by many other factors, some of which the mind of man may recognize: the relationship of the earth to the sun, for instance, is a primary factor. So there is something specific which can occur in this planet and which has obviously occurred, but what has taken place was drawn to point from out of the cosmic whole. So we may see the Father, over all, and something which may be designated by the term "the Son," a specific essence derived from the Father. This finds expression and manifestation by reason of life's design and purpose, in the natural form which it takes on this particular planet.

This, of course, does not deny the design and purpose revealed elsewhere in the cosmos in specific patterns of expression and manifestation. So we certainly are not to assume that this stands unique here on earth, as though nothing of a similar nature could take place anywhere else. However, the form of the design and purpose will vary according to the conditions. We have these conditions on earth, so we have this form. We do not need to concern ourselves with the conditions elsewhere at the moment, and therefore with the forms elsewhere; we have enough to do here. Man is inclined to have the habit, individually speaking, of minding other people's business. This habit is also prevalent collectively speaking. He tries to mind the business where he has no business: reaching out into space. This is looked upon by man as progress. It could be looked upon as trespassing. "Forgive us our trespasses, as we forgive those who trespass against us." It could also be looked upon as evidence of imminent disaster, because the clever mind of man is now able to do so much that violates the cosmic design and purpose of life. The more he violates that design and purpose, the more quickly the reaction comes back upon his own head by reason of the working of the Law. So the fact is that no one ever gets away with anything. Mankind as a whole certainly doesn't, nor do we individually.

If we begin to align ourselves with life and its design and purposes, so that this is our motivation, then the future, the disastrous future, may be changed. But if we continue, with the rest of mankind, along the path of blindness—self-seeking, trying to fulfil personal desires and wants—then, with the rest, we perish. God the Father is not willing that any should perish, but that all should come to repentance, that all should be willing to change their ways so that the clever mind ceases to direct the course of human events. The human mind in self-activity multiplies problems until they finally overwhelm. Some who have begun to see this think that the solution would be to reverse the direction. However, the fact of the matter is that it is irreversible; you can't go back to the simple life of five miles per hour.

What is it that is needed? Only that we cease to allow the human mind to govern us, that we cut off what has been described as self-activity. Personal desire, even though it seems very good, is included in what needs to go. The translation of the human mind of what seems to be required to allow man to continue to exist on the surface of this planet—all that needs to go, because life has design, it has purpose, waiting to be accepted exactly as it is, without any manipulation or adjustment to suit human beings. Human function is almost entirely based upon what the individual thinks he wants: "I want this sort of a life. I want to design my life in this way because I think it will suit me. This would be more pleasing to me. This would satisfy me, and if I am satisfied then I will be of more value in the world." To do what? To add to the chaos and the destructiveness? Is that value?

Does anyone know what life's design and purpose for him is? You may know that life has a design and purpose for you, but what is it? The mind gets busy and says, "Well, I think this would be nice. I think I could be really effective there, and I like to do that, so I am going in this direction—like it or not!" We have confusion and chaos as a result—everybody trying to do what is good in his own eyes. That is a violation of integrity; that is dishonesty. And while it may be dressed up to look fairly pleasing to human eyes sometimes, underneath it's rotten. As our Master put it: "whited sepulchres, full of dead men's bones, and all uncleanness." This is the state of those who are governed by their own desires, by their own determinations, ignoring the design and purpose of life itself. The design and purpose of life itself springs from the Father. Do you imagine that any puny little human being is going to frustrate the design and purpose of the Father, the design and purpose which takes form in the cosmic whole? That would be ridiculous! All that happens is that the puny human being is swept out of the way—dust to dust, ashes to ashes.

But life's design and purpose are present. They will not be frustrated. If human beings feel frustrated they may know why: because they are not with it; they are not allowing the experience of life's design and purpose to be known by themselves; they are standing in the way of it. Life's design and purpose is one thing; it is not a multitude of separate things. The cosmos is one thing, a whole; it is not a multitude of separate things. There are many parts to that one whole, but they are all parts of the one whole. The design and

purpose of the whole are supreme. Only as the design
and purpose of the whole are brought specifically to
point in the part, does that part survive. We have a responsibility in this part, this earth, this world, the responsibility to bring to focus the design and purpose
of the cosmic whole as it applies here. This is why it is
true, according to the statement, that man was made
in the image and likeness of God, capable of allowing
life's design and purpose to be brought to focus here,
out of the cosmic whole, that the beauty of that design
and purpose might take form in manifestation on
earth, to the glory of God.

The mind doesn't know this; the mind doesn't know
what it would be. The mind doesn't comprehend anything of itself. It is part of the evidence of the presence of life's design and purpose. It has a place in that
design and purpose, but it is certainly not there to try
to determine what the design and purpose should be.
The mind of man would not even exist if life did not
have a design and a purpose. Let it begin to yield to
that design and purpose, relinquishing its arrogance,
for there is nothing that the mind can do, no knowledge that it can acquire, that will serve any purpose
other than that of destruction, as long as it continues
to try to direct the course of life. To what end the increase of knowledge? That destruction may come
more quickly, that's all. When life's design and purpose control, then knowledge may be useful, but not
before. Which is more important, then, that we should
multiply knowledge or that we should rediscover what
it is to be governed by life's design and purpose? This
latter is repentance—turning again to God. What a
naive suggestion! At least it seems that way to the ar-
rogant human mind. God has been discredited long
ago! Has He really? How interesting! I wonder what it
is that has really been discredited. "The prince of this
world *is* judged." The mind of man *is* judged—weighed

in the balance and found wanting, found basically stupid, exalting its own knowledge as though sufficient could be gained to enable man to direct the course of life in the cosmic whole. Life belongs to the cosmic whole, not to man. Let it reveal itself in the true expression of the cosmic whole, brought to focus here on earth, and the so-called problems produced by the human mind vanish as though they had never been, for it is the human mind itself which keeps them in existence within the range of its own consciousness.

From the standpoint of the Father, from the standpoint of the cosmic whole, man's problems don't exist. They are meaningless; they don't need solving. How much energy human beings channel into endeavors to solve their problems! They don't need solving. There isn't any solution, because the problems themselves are the pipe dreams of the mind of man, produced by the mind of man, maintained by the mind of man, which multiplies them by trying to solve them, and yet it doesn't see how stupid it is. Let us emerge out of that jungle because we cease having faith in the king of beasts. There are things that are going on in the jungle which should be going on in the jungle, but man doesn't belong in the jungle. Rising up above the jungle, there may be a new viewpoint, a new outlook, a new understanding. But it is impossible to rise up out of the jungle as long as the conscious mind dominates the individual, as long as he imagines he is wise in his own eyes, as long as he thinks he knows what's good or what's bad, as long as he thinks he can direct what he calls his own life. The very fact that he calls it his own life reveals that he is a thief, a thief and a robber. The world of man is a den of thieves, instead of being a house of prayer.

Our Father which art in heaven, hallowed be *Thy* name—not the name of the human intellect. *Thy* kingdom come. *Thy* will be done in earth, as it is in heaven. Here is the open door to mankind, the open door to every individual upon the face of the earth. Who shall come through it? Who shall yield to life's design and purpose? Who shall relinquish personal desire and interpretation of purpose? As there are those who are so willing, then the fact that God the Father is not willing that any should perish will become known and experienced. Here is the way, the truth and the life for all who will receive it.

Potential Released

Whenever a new baby form comes into the world there are, as a rule, great expectations for the child. There is a recognition of potential. How very seldom, though, is the potential adequately realized in the subsequent experience of life. If we stop to consider the matter we would have to recognize that there could be considerable disappointment from the standpoint of the Lord. Sometimes parents are disappointed in their children, but think of the tremendous possibilities from the divine standpoint—and the little damp squib that goes off in the expression of human life, so called. It is a sad, sad thing. But I think most people, even though they may not have any conscious awareness of the real extent of their own potentiality, nevertheless have an inherent feeling of depression with respect to the small amount of that potential which puts in an appearance in actual fact.

Where there is some measure of manifestation insofar as the possibilities are concerned in a person it is a wonderful thing, isn't it? There is no real reason why the fulness should not appear. If we are honorable people we are concerned that it should, and we will not do anything to prevent it. It does require some deliberate action to prevent it. Usually we have thought of the deliberate action as relating to what is necessary to let it appear. It is true there is need for some action in that regard, but if it is prevented it takes deliberate action on the part of a person. It is not something that just happens, for from the divine standpoint everything that is essential to the unfoldment of that individual's true expression of life is present. It is present with every person on the face of the earth. If that potential does not find full realization it is because it has been deliberately prevented.

Perhaps we do not need to dwell particularly on this aspect of the matter but it should be recognized as a fact, because there are endless excuses in human hearts for failure in this regard. The excuses are rather hollow. Such failure is consequent upon the individual's own deliberate choice to resist that divine potential which is pressing to come forth. Sometimes we say we are here to let the Lord reveal Himself through us. Then the human ego rises up and says, "Well, that doesn't give me a chance to express *my*self." Who are you? As long as we set the Lord over in the corner somewhere and imagine we are so important that we must be in position to let Him express, we have a very self-centered and unreasonable attitude, because we recall that the name of the Lord, insofar as each person is concerned, is "I AM," and it is the individual's own true expression which is divine and which reveals the Lord. It is not some disembodied expression coming from somewhere to occupy the human form and to reveal itself without regard to the individual, as such. The revelation is of the person himself, or herself. It is not of someone else. It is the revelation of one's own potential, of all that is locked up within oneself. Yet, how strenuously people insist upon blocking that expression, hiding it away, shackling it. There are always such good reasons for doing it, in the individual's own mind, but when that is done a person is destroying himself. If you destroy the expression of yourself on earth, is that not destroying yourself? Eventually the expression ceases altogether, and then that is looked upon as death. The suppression of oneself is the process of dying. The process of living is the release of oneself, the willingness to allow that which he divinely is to break through the barriers and to come forth in the brilliant expression of divine being which is natural to the person.

Sometimes there is rebellion against the use of the word "divine," and the person says, "Oh, I don't want to be divine." If you don't want to be divine you want to be dead, and of course there are those people who reach the point where they have so sat on their true expression of themselves that they say, "I wish I were dead." Well, it's not far off. To reach a point where one has such an attitude is very obvious evidence that the person has refused to allow his own true expression to appear on earth. He has, we might say, been playing the fool, hasn't he? Playing the fool! There are so many people playing the fool.

A distinction is made in some of the Old Testament passages between the wise man and the fool. The wise man is the individual who reveals himself, and the fool is the individual who suppresses himself—suppresses himself by deliberately establishing a pretense, by deliberately taking attitudes which establish a counterfeit in expression. One of the attitudes that is very prevalent in this regard is the attitude which may be described as reluctance. Of course, perhaps it may be said that there are those things that we should be a little reluctant about, but in the general pattern of existence, as human beings know it, we may easily observe those who are reluctant to do what comes to hand to do. They have an attitude which proclaims, perhaps, "Who are you to ask me to do this?" or, "I can't really be bothered." The reluctant attitude is one of the best ways of shackling oneself. Of course, the person usually takes such an attitude in an endeavor to be nasty to someone else. He thinks he is revealing his own superiority over someone else, but actually when a reluctant attitude is taken the individual is simply preventing the expression of himself. He is locking the door.

We have spoken of the vital importance of what is called willingness. Mention was made the other day of the derivation of the word "belief": be-lief. "Lief" is an old English word which was commonly used in years gone by, and indicates something with respect to willingness, so that "be-lief" could be translated as "be-willing." Be willing! What a tremendous quality this is. It is one of the primary qualities present in a person which will begin to release that person, release him from the prison of his own making. Now, we are all prisoners to some degree, to start with, but it is in the willingness that we find release. There is so much of the "dog-in-the-manger" attitude in the world of man. For instance, if you were employed by someone in the world pattern to do some certain job, the usual approach is—I trust it wouldn't be yours—"I'm not going to do more than I have to, just enough to get by and get my pay check." Of course, if you take it too far, then you lose your pay check. So there is a fine line here. The individual spends most of his life endeavoring to walk this tightrope—not enough to get fired but not enough to be of any real value, and the thought is, "I don't have to give more of myself than this to this person." The idea is that one is then asserting one's independence in relationship to the boss. But what is the person really doing? He is strangling himself. He may be hurting the boss a little, but if he hurts the boss too much he is going to lose his job anyway.

The point is, how ridiculous to spend one's life strangling oneself. Could there be anything more stupid? Here is a wonderful opportunity to begin to allow oneself to come forth, and how human beings set up this facade in front of themselves and dare other people to find them. And it is interesting how kind many people are in making allowances for others, in order to help them, as they think. Sometimes it does, of course, but generally speaking it would be much more helpful if the individual had a good swift kick in the pants. Of course, the very self-centered person then says, "Well, look, I'm being ill-treated," and builds up his defenses still more, tightening the knot around his own neck. Yet, present within everyone there is this potential. It is there. How insane to spend one's days throttling it, refusing to let it come forth, and is this not deliberate action? Of course it is. The person says, "No, I won't. I won't give more of myself. I don't see why I should." Well, if you don't see why you should, you could see why it is most unwise to continue to prevent it, because here is how human beings commit suicide, and spend their lives in utter misery. It is not a happy state. How could it be? But when we become willing to give more of ourselves than is asked and more of ourselves than we think we are able, something begins to open up. Something begins to come out, and we begin to discover that we are far more able than we thought. We find that our potential has scarcely been glimpsed. We may know it is there but we don't know what it is until it comes forth. There is the inherent awareness in everyone, actually, of potential. Sometimes the individual, in order to avoid bringing it forth —such avoidance is stupidity, isn't it?—may depreciate himself to himself, saying, "I'm not really worth anything." Of course, usually when a person says that, he is trying to persuade someone to tell him that he is worth something, or to convince him somehow that he is worth something. Well, he is worth something potentially, and it is true of everyone, but as long as it remains merely a potential, of what earthly value is it? A person may sit inside himself and say, "Ah, I know I'm worth something in here," but in fact he is worth nothing out there. The value locked up inside goes to waste insofar as any experience on earth is concerned. It is only when it comes out in the pattern of living that we begin to discover the wonder of it, the glory of it, and we begin to have some real self-respect.

The individual who is reluctant, in the sense in which I have outlined it, despises himself. Whatever he may say, his hangdog attitude is evidence of self-despising. He has no respect for himself. It is the potential being brought forth into living expression that brings with it an awareness of one's own value, of one's own worth, and therefore there is a natural self-respect—and one cannot be happy without self-respect.

Such tremendous potential is locked up within each baby form born into this world. With the world the way it is, there is a tendency to bind the child in swaddling clothes in an attempt to prevent that potential from appearing. Of course, that is not the attitude that the parents take, but it is the fact, generally speaking, by reason of what they do. We may recall that in the story of our Master's birth He was wrapped in swaddling clothes, round, and round, and round, but it did not stop that which He was from coming forth, and there is nothing that can stop this coming forth except the individual's own attitude. It is popular to imagine that one has been prevented from experiencing potential by reason of all the terrible things that were done in one's upbringing, and then, later on, the circumstances of life, the envyings and the jealousies, and all the other things which human beings accept as excuses for failing to be what they know they should be. But the only reason for failure is one's own attitude, that alone. And it is the course of wisdom, and an indication of the beginnings of maturity, to acknowledge this. Human beings are their own worst enemies.

The adversary is—where? Usually even responding ones are inclined to look around, look under the bed and in the closet to find the adversary. They talk about the mass consciousness and the evil points of focus in the world, black magicians and whatnots—all out there somewhere. If they are just out there, that's fine. Leave them out there. They can't touch you as long as they are out there. These things only begin to touch a person when they are in here, when they are what one is oneself. You have no other enemy but yourself. And what was the Master's instruction? "Love your enemies." If you don't respect yourself you don't like yourself, and regardless of what you think with your conscious mind about yourself your actions and your attitudes will reveal what the state of affairs really is. If you don't like yourself you are subject to your enemy; your enemy is in charge, and you are your enemy, and an enemy is interested in defeating. So, we have you interested in defeating yourself, and of course that is the experience. As our Master said, "A house divided against itself cannot stand," and it doesn't. It collapses. It disintegrates. But if we begin to love our enemy we don't have any enemy anymore, and we begin to deliberately do those things which will allow the increased release of what we are in the expression of life, and what we are is divine. And "divine" is a wonderful word. It means something wonderful. It may have meant something not so acceptable in the consciousness of fallen human beings sometimes, but the word "divine" really means something that is absolutely wonderful, entirely acceptable, something that brings joy and happiness, something which allows fulfilment in life, all for which the individual really longs, even though he may spend his days strangling himself.

Be willing. Believe in God. Believe in yourself. Believe in your own potential, and that means be willing to allow your potential to appear so that you may know what it is, and everyone else may too. As long as we have potential all locked up inside it is of no value to us, and no one else knows what it is. If we are insisting that everyone else around us should have such keen spiritual vision that they can penetrate the armor we have put up, and find our potential inside, and say, "Aren't you wonderful!" we are being rather silly, I think, because we find that most people, in any case, are interested in themselves and not in you. However, let's bring it forth, and then it can be seen, and as our Master said, "A city that is set on an hill cannot be hid."

If what you are comes forth, people will know it, and some will delight in it. Others won't like it too much, but it will be known anyway. Of what value is it to go through life as a nonentity? We may be known for that which we are if we are willing that this potential should come forth. As long as we are reluctant in our function it never comes forth. There are those who insist upon some narrow little field through which they are willing that it should come forth, but of course what comes forth through that is not anything of real meaning or moment. It must include the whole person and everything with which one is dealing. If you are reluctant in certain fields you are strangling yourself because of it, even though you may be a little bit willing in some other fields. And I have noted a pattern of this nature even within the scope of our own program: a certain willingness in certain chosen fields, where the individual says, "Well, I want to do that, so I'm going to be willing"; but if he doesn't want to do it: "Oh, no! Not me." There is a reluctance and a throttling of the individual himself by himself, and we never know anything worthwhile through that person, even though there may be a little range of willingness in the area where he wants to be willing. But that does not reveal anything divine. That reveals the human want, that is all.

If it is divine it includes everything, and one is willing in every field. Now, it may be that in certain fields one may not yet have the required ability in the external sense, and certainly in such case there needs to be caution, but the caution is because one is developing ability, not because one is not willing. There are those who have been foolish in this regard. They have said, "I'm willing to do anything," and they will rush in where angels fear to tread. Because they don't have the ability they make an infernal mess and confusion in consequence. Whereas if they had approached it with caution they could have learned as they went along, and then their willingness would have had some meaning in that field. On the other hand there are those who say, "Well, I don't have any ability in that direction; therefore I'm not willing; I won't," and there is very definite reluctance in such case, more than reluctance. But one can learn. There is a saying that you can't teach an old dog new tricks. That may be true of dogs! But let us not classify ourselves with dogs. And the tricks are not new, anyway. They are the expression of what we are, and that is not new; that is eternal.

As there is willingness, deliberate willingness instead of deliberate reluctance, we begin to allow potential to have meaning. Something comes forth of what we are. The individual who has a reluctant attitude is most dissatisfied with what he is. He doesn't like it, but he just continues to strangle himself. How foolish! We can change. We can let the potential which appeared on earth in the baby form when we came first into the world be realized. Think of all the millions and billions of human beings who have been born into the world, lived their little life span, and the potential that was present has simply never been known. Think of the loss. If any human being in the human pattern of things tried to operate his business on that basis he would be bankrupt in no time. That is why the world is so bankrupt: because the riches of divine potential have been frustrated in their expression on earth. And that divine potential is not something separate from human beings. It is what they are. It is, with respect to oneself, one's own reality, one's own being, that which one is. Why should we be afraid of it? Why should we resist it? Why should we fight it? Why should we attempt to destroy it? Rather, let us concern ourselves with finding out what that potential is.

Whenever an individual begins to let this come forth, what a wonderful delight it is. It certainly is a joy to me, and I know it is a joy to all of you when you see it appearing through someone—provided you are not too wrapped up in your own state of strangulation. It is wonderful to see it appearing through someone else, and it is wonderful to have the experience through oneself. You discover that there is no real limit to what you are.

And so, we should remember these things, and give a little thought to the extent to which we have been willing to let our own potential be realized, to let ourselves be revealed on earth, to ourselves and to others. Let us not so function that we are a disappointment to the Lord, or to anyone else for that matter. It is a most devastating thing to disappoint oneself, and it is because human beings are doing that most of the time that they find they are in a state of devastation. Moving willingly in all the fields of our daily function, let us give what we are into them, so that we may find out what we are—no reluctance, no holding back, no limitations arbitrarily imposed upon ourselves, but an opening up, a birth, a bringing forth. This is fulfilment, isn't it? It might take quite a while to experience all the fulfilment, but we find joy in doing it.

The Art of Peace in a World of War

"The Art of Peace in a World of War." These are challenging words and could bear considerable meditation, more than we could possibly give them in this brief time. Yet how vital it is that we should give consideration to them, and see what we might learn.

We do live in a world of war; perhaps at the moment not an active, fighting war insofar as we here are concerned, although there is that sort of activity going on in different places where people are fighting. Much effort has been made to put an end to war but I do not think any of it gives any particular assurance that there will be no war. If we simply look to the leaders of the world, the governments of the world, to do what is necessary to establish a state of peace, I would suggest that we will be looking in vain and deluding ourselves. No human leader anywhere, no government anywhere, can in fact establish a state of peace. If the Canadian government passed some legislation tomorrow making a state of peace in Canada the law of the land, would that produce a state of peace in you? Obviously, tranquility of mind and heart cannot be produced by legislation, by acts of government, or by the pronouncement of leaders. I certainly do not anticipate that anything I might say at this time will, of itself, establish a state of peace in you. Perhaps you have already experienced such a condition, in which case I rejoice; but if you have not as yet, adequately at least, then it will not be produced by anything I might say. Perhaps for the moment there may be something of the possibility of experiencing a certain peacefulness, but to have any meaning it needs to stay with us.

The world is full of conflict. Individual human lives are full of conflict. There could not possibly be a state of peace in the world as long as there are nations vying with one another, for whatever reason; but, when we stop to consider the matter, obviously the nations of the world are made up of people, and people include you and me. If there is to be a peaceful world it must be by reason of something that you and I do. It is utterly hopeless simply to look to the leaders and the governments of the world to produce peace for us. It cannot be done.

Looking at the world situation dispassionately, what activity that has been undertaken on an international scale gives promise of producing a peaceful state in the world? Is there anything that we could pin our hopes on? I do not think there is. We have disarmament conferences, but even if they were successful, which does not seem at all likely in any case, would that produce a state of peace? I do not think so. Perhaps you yourselves have experienced in your own lives a state of conflict in relationship to others which was not a battle in the sense of coming to blows, and yet there was a very definite state of conflict, a feeling of tension and discomfort, something most unpleasant inside. A state of conflict! And just because we do not have a gun handy to shoot the one with whom the conflict is engendered—and perhaps other reasons may restrain our hands—it certainly does not mean that we immediately experience a state of peace. It goes on boiling inside. Nations are made up of human beings—you and me—and what we do is of vital moment. I suppose we might say, "Well, we are more or less insignificant people, living in a little corner of the world. The world is a big place; there are a lot of people in it. What difference could it make what we do?" I wonder. If we could see something, and recognize that there was something we could do, and we proceeded to do it, then at least there would be a few people on earth who were actually doing something to produce what is required. If we here, and others in other places, just sit down and wait for someone else to do something, or expect the leaders of the world to get together somehow, we are liable to wait in vain—in fact it would be a certainty if everybody did it.

Let us consider this matter of peace and war. What is peace? Is it just the absence of something, the absence of war, the absence of conflict? Many people seem to look on it that way. All the efforts that are made to establish peace are based upon endeavors to eliminate war, as though once you had eliminated the war, peace would be there automatically. Is that actually the case?

I suppose we could use an analogy to make a point here. What is darkness? Is it merely the absence of light, or is light something of itself and darkness merely the evidence of the absence of the light? If we think of war—or shall we call it "conflict"?—as being a state of darkness, then how are we going to get rid of the darkness? Are we going to get rid of it by talking about it, by arguing about it, by conferences with respect to it? We cannot get rid of the darkness by any means except by introducing light.

There is the story of the gentleman who was in the mental institution, who used to spend the whole night with a bucket, baling the darkness out of the window; and then, with a sigh of relief, he would see the sun rising in the morning and say, "Well, at last I've got rid of the darkness."

We cannot get rid of war, we cannot get rid of con-

flict, by struggling with the conflict and with the war.
It will never be eliminated by eliminating armaments.
I suppose, conceivably, it could be eliminated by eliminating human beings; but then there would be no one
present to know the meaning of peace. Peace *is* something, and it should never be looked upon as merely
the absence of conflict. Most people who have turmoil
inside themselves are inclined to want to get rid of it.
They want to get rid of that uncomfortable feeling.
They are distraught, frustrated—"What can we *do* to
get rid of this?" We can struggle with it, we can analyze it, spend our whole lives considering states of
frustration, turmoil and distortion of all kinds that
may be present in human lives. We may learn a lot
about such things. There is, for instance, the study of
the art of war. But we will never get rid of conflict or
war by any such means, will we?

If our analogy does hold good, the only way that
darkness or conflict can be caused to depart is to introduce the light, or the state of peace. We need to think
about peace, and what it is, so that we may play a part
in permitting that state to appear. If that state is here,
then the state of conflict is not here. But to try to dis-
pose of the state of conflict without recognizing the
fact of a true state of peace, something of itself, is impossible; it just leaves a blank. We get rid of our conflicts, and what will be left? Of course, we cannot get
rid of our conflicts that way, except by dying perhaps,
and then what is there left? We need to recognize the
somethingness of a state of peace, so that we can concern ourselves with that state and turn our attention
away from this business of trying to get rid of war, trying to get rid of conflict.

In the world of man there are a great many organi-
zations which are "agin" something—anti-something
leagues of all kinds. The so-called Western world at
the present time has seemed to be principally anti-

communist. But what are we *for?* We can find all
sorts of things that we are against—that is not hard at
all. There are lots of things we do not like, things that
are uncomfortable, etc. This state of turmoil, of conflict, is one of them. Are we simply going to be an anti-
war league? What would be achieved? Actually, by
such anti attitudes we support the very thing we are
against. Our thoughts, our actions, our energies, our
life force, all are channeled into this business of being
against something; and whatever it is that we are
against profits thereby, to the extent of our life force,
whatever energy we put into it. Wrong things are
never eliminated that way. They may change their
names or their shapes a little.

It was not so long ago that we fought a war against
something that was called fascism, or the Nazi ideology. We were victorious. Wonderful! Congratulations!
We do not have any more Nazis, at the moment at
least, causing trouble. There may be some round
about but they do not cause us too much disturbance
at the moment. However, we have something else in
its place; they call it communism. There is a tape re-
corder here, and if it works the way I believe it does,
when you press down one button another button
comes up. That is the way things work. We can be
anti something and we can push it down. All kinds of
things have been pushed down from the standpoint of
the medical field. Great victories have been won over
different diseases. Things that used to scourge mankind not so long ago have been brought under control
apparently, but as fast as they are brought under control something else pops up. We get inoculated or vaccinated for one thing, and we find we have to be inoculated or vaccinated for half a dozen others, if that is
the way to deal with the situation. The point is that
being against things accomplishes nothing. We have
the ability to change the world's furniture around, so

to speak, but it is all still there; nothing has been accomplished. Something needs to be introduced. We need to be *for* something, rather than simply against things in general. I suppose the path of least resistance is in relationship to the things we can so easily be against. But it takes something to be *for* something.

We need to recognize, in relationship to this particular field of consideration, that it is the state of peace itself which is what we should be for, so that we may stop being so concerned about all the things that produce conflict and begin to concern ourselves with those things which produce peace. This is something we need to look at, obviously, from an individual standpoint. As I pointed out before, just to expect someone out there somewhere—leaders, governments—to do what is required and produce the state of peace is, at best, blindness, because it can never be done on that basis. It is only as there are some human beings somewhere who permit peace, or the state of peace, to be established in relationship to themselves, that peace can be introduced into the world. We look around and see this state of conflict everywhere. It gives, like darkness, the evidence of the absence of something. Darkness is the evidence of the absence of light. All we have to do is introduce the light, and the darkness will go. Where did it go? It really was not anything, actually; just the absence of something. And so it is with conflict, turmoil. All these tiresome things which plague human beings are not really anything of themselves; they just give evidence of the fact that something is not there that should be there. Well, let us find out what should be there and play our part in letting it be produced.

When we begin to discover what peace is, then we could be classified among those who would be called "peacemakers." If you came across two human beings battling together—assuming that you were physically able to separate them—would that resolve all their differences? It would not, would it? You would have to introduce something, something which was sufficiently strong to claim the attention of the contestants, so that they would, for the moment at least, forget their differences and look at something else. Now, of course, in a rather backhanded way this occurs when we go to war. Fear unites people for the moment because they are afraid they are going to lose something. Then, as human beings, we are inclined to pull together because that thing of which we are afraid looms so large that our differences are forgotten. They are still there but they are overlooked for the moment. Fear is not a very constructive basis for producing peace, is it? People who are afraid are not at peace. Something else is needed, something that is strong enough of itself, not only to claim the attention of those who otherwise might be in a state of conflict but also to provide that which is necessary to produce the state of peace. Again, it is not simply a matter of getting rid of the conflict, is it? Something positive, something real and strong, must appear if the state of peace is to be experienced. How shall we find it? Where will we look? What is it that really produces the discord inside a person? Again, of course, we can always look around and see our neighbor over there, or perhaps even husband or wife, or mother-in-law, someone else, some circumstance, and we say, "Well, there's the reason now! If I could just get rid of that, then everything would be wonderful." Did you ever succeed in producing a state that was wonderful on that basis? No, because it is impossible. There may be alleviation of difficulty for the moment but it will crop up again, somehow, somewhere, through someone or through some circumstance. Why? Because basically the trouble is inside the person himself, not out there.

I heard rather a nice little story the other day in this

connection. It was told by a man from India. It is about a rich man and a robber, and the rich man was going to travel from one city to another. He went by train. Quite some years ago in India the banking system was not operating perhaps as it does now; in any case, there was the necessity of taking his cash with him. He had fifty thousand dollars. The robber became aware of the fact that the rich man was going to travel with this fifty thousand dollars, so he proceeded to attach himself to the rich man, and when he bought a ticket to this other city the robber bought one too. And when the rich man got into a compartment, the robber got into the same compartment, and he proceeded to make friends with the rich man. He bought him breakfast, lunch, tea, supper. He thought it was a good investment, I suppose. Then just before retiring he went out of the compartment to get a glass of milk for the rich man; went back in, and they settled themselves down for the night. It was a two-day journey, incidentally. When the rich man fell asleep—perhaps the robber put something in his milk, I do not know—he slept sufficiently soundly so that the robber searched in his bag; in his other bag; in his pockets; everywhere; he could not find the money. This, of course, was very disappointing to him. He felt badly, and decided that, well, he would excuse himself the next day and leave the train; it was no use; apparently he did not have the money anyway.

So the next morning he thought, well perhaps he had better buy breakfast again for the rich man so as to taper off their acquaintance easily, and went out of the compartment. When he came back, here was the rich man counting his money—a big wad of fifty thousand dollars. The robber could hardly believe his eyes. "Well! He still has it. I'll try again tonight." So he went through the same procedure again, and fetched him his glass of milk in the evening. The rich man went to sleep. The robber proceeded to search again. He went through everything. He even took his shoes off and looked in the soles of his shoes—everywhere! No sign of the money anywhere. A terrible disappointment.

In the morning the rich man thanked his acquaintance for the care he had taken of him on the train, and he took out a card and said, "If ever you are in this city, be sure to call upon me." The robber was really a little disturbed, and he said, "There is one question I would like to ask you." The rich man said, "Go ahead! Go ahead!" He said, "Well, I'm a robber, and I've robbed people all my life, and I came on this train to rob you. I knew you had the money, and I searched last night and the night before, and I couldn't find it anywhere. Where do you keep your money?" So the rich man said, "When I got on the train I was a little concerned about you. I suspected you might be a robber, and I was afraid of losing my money. I was afraid that you might stick a knife in me too. So I took precautions." The robber said, "Well, what did you do? Where did you put the money, that I couldn't find it?" He said, "I hid it under your pillow."

That is a wonderful story, actually. Human beings are always looking at someone else. They do not look under their own pillow. The statement which the rich man made was this: "I thought you were clever enough to search everywhere, in my clothes and bags, but I thought you were fool enough not to look under your own pillow!" Let us not be equally foolish, because if there is trouble in the world it is not "out there," insofar as we personally are concerned. It is right here, under our own pillow; and when we become wise enough to look at what it is that is under our own pillow, then we can be of value in learning the true art of peace, because we will not foolishly be projecting the things that are actually inside ourselves onto others, so as to get them away from ourselves.

We need to recognize that there is something that needs to change in us, regardless of what happens in anyone else, if there is ever to be a state of peace on earth.

Human beings know the state of war, the state of conflict. You know what it is, do you not, without exception, every one of you? All of us together—we know what it is. We have been through the mill, and are still going through the mill in one way or another —conflict, turmoil, disturbance, unhappiness. We know that state. Because we know that state so well, it is evident that we do not know the state of peace. We cannot have them both at the same time. You cannot have darkness and light in the same place at the same time. When the light is turned on, the darkness is gone. When we recognize that there is that present in relationship to ourselves which is capable of experiencing the state of peace, so that we do something about it, then the light begins to shine and the darkness is gone. We did not have to struggle with it. We did not have to analyze it, try to push it out of ourselves, get rid of it. We did not have to do a thing about it.

Here we have a world looking for peace. Some have this notion, and some that. I suppose the communists imagine that if once the world is all communized, then everything will be peaceful. Will it? A childish fancy! On the other hand, I suppose the so-called free world imagines, "If we could just get rid of communism, then everything would be peaceful." Would it? Of course not! We are not going to find some magic formula to produce a state of peace in the world of mankind until we ourselves have individually found it in relationship to ourselves. Then there is the magic formula—not through somebody else, by reason of what someone else did, but by reason of something that we did. This conflict, this turmoil, this state of unhappiness that human beings know, is by reason of something in themselves. Oh, it is so easy—it is so easy! to see that it is what someone does out there that is all the trouble, is it not? But it is *not*. It is what is going on inside ourselves that is the trouble. You know that some things bother you that do not bother your neighbor at all. It is not the things; it is what happens inside us that is the trouble; and when we begin to let something happen inside us that produces the state of peace, then we know what it is, and the state of conflict is gone. But it is something that happens inside oneself.

There is a conflict inside. It is, as it were, that we have two natures—one which is known by the state of turmoil, conflict; one which is known by reason of a state of peace. These two natures inside are basically the cause of conflict. There is a tendency in what is called the Christian world to emphasize the sinfulness of human beings. "They are all wrong—terrible!" Well, obviously there are some things wrong with people. Even, it may be there is something wrong with us. But could it be that there is also something right with people? I think so. If we are all the time so desperately concerned about the things that are wrong, then we are struggling with the darkness; and we stay wrong, no matter what we do. It is quite an effort to try to be good, you know—have you discovered that?—quite an effort to try to conform to the popular idea of what constitutes a good person. There is a sort of model, is there not, which people are supposed to emulate, a model which is established on the basis of the particular society in which we live. It is not the same the world around. It depends on where you live, what your religion is, etc. There is a certain ideal which is presented, and you must conform with that to be good. But are we all supposed to be the same? Is this idea going to fit everybody? I do not think, in actual fact, it fits anyone. It is just a figment of fancy, anyway. There is that which a person really is, inside. Maybe that is covered up a good deal by something plastered on the outside, but it is there, and it is right. It is what the person actually is. I do not think that is something to suppress in order to try to conform with some social or religious idea, a product of the human mind. There *is* something, in relationship to everyone, that is right. It is there. It is present. It is what you really are. But you were brought up in this world of man, and you were trained to try to conform to the pattern that had been laid down, and the pattern to which you were trying to conform did not allow the expression of what you really were, and so—conflict! There you were, trying to conform to something, and inside there was something rebellious perhaps, something that was not comfortable inside to conform to that. Conflict! That is basically the reason for all conflict. In order to get this discomfort out from inside it is convenient to blame somebody else, out there. "If they would just behave themselves out there, then I would be all right." But that does not work either, because the trouble actually originates inside; and when we begin to recognize this we have a key.

Of course, most people manage somehow to get by in life, conforming more or less to the established requirements, but there are those who suffer the consequences, one way or another. We have criminal activity: the conflict becomes extreme and the individual tries to break out of the established norm, to which all the good people are supposed to conform, and tries to make some other pattern for himself. But that is not right either. We have so-called juvenile delinquency. We have neurotic tendencies of all kinds based fundamentally on this one thing—a human being trying to conform to a pattern in which he does not fit. And in the world, with things the way they are in this world of war, we are told, "Well, the solution to that is to become objective. You adjust to the world of war, to the world of conflict, so that you can manage to retain your balance somehow while in a state of unhappiness, turmoil and conflict." But that is not any solution.

The state of peace is the natural state in relationship to you as you really are inside. When what you really are inside is allowed to come out, you know that state of peace, wherever you may be. Peace comes from inside. It cannot be plastered on the outside, and it is a natural state. It is not something that you can get. It is something that is true now in relationship to each one —all of you here, everyone on the face of the earth actually. That which the individual actually is, inside, naturally experiences a state of peace. Most people are so involved in the state of war that they never become aware of what they really are. They are in this conflict, battle, going back and forth, trying to keep their heads above water, so to speak, in a difficult world, and they never find out what they really are. There is no possibility of the experience of the state of peace on earth without human beings discovering that which they really are inside. Let us not accept any idea that says that human beings are sinners, wrong all the way through. Nonsense!

Some ideas in the Christian world have been expressed with respect to the so-called fall of man: Adam and Eve partook of the forbidden fruit, and consequently everyone ever since has been hopelessly and helplessly enslaved by this evil nature. Man's real nature is not evil. I think, if we give any thought to the matter from the standpoint of something that a divine creator would make, he would not make something that was evil, wrong, rotten. I do not think so. There is that which is right, and we need to recognize there is that which is right and begin to discover what we really are, and let that come out, because it is only as we do so that we can discover the art of peace. The art of peace is the art of living, and there is no living for any until they let that which is right inside of their true nature come out. We may imagine that we can manipulate the things out here to get everything set just the way we like it, and everything will be fine! But it does not work. And if you succeeded in doing that in your environment, then presumably everybody else would be miserable because they would not be getting things just the way *they* wanted them; and if we are all trying to get things just the way we want them, then there is going to be conflict and confusion, turmoil and war.

The state of peace is already inside; we cannot get it from any external source; but when we begin to let it come out from inside, then it begins to change things round about. There begins to be the reality of a state of peace on earth. There begins to be that which is analogous to light on earth. Where the light is, the darkness is gone. It is really very simple but we need to see it for ourselves, so that it is not just a matter of theory with respect to someone else, or some other time, some other place, but we begin to see it in relationship to ourselves here and now. And we begin to have confidence in what we truly are. Most people, not being aware of what they truly are, are desperately afraid. Have you ever noticed how touchy people are?—always on the defensive, afraid they are going to lose themselves somehow. But they have never found themselves. We need to find ourselves, not simply as human beings in a state of war, conflict, turmoil, but as something divine in a state of peace. When we do find ourselves that way, then we have, to that extent, played a part in making peace on earth—which is more than any of the leaders of the world have been able to do thus far, is it not?

Which, then, would be more important? A leader

out there somewhere who is trying to produce a state
in which there is no war, or you, right where you are,
actually making peace? I think you would be far more
important, because the solution would be appearing
through you, not through that person out there, no
matter what he did, unless he started to participate in
the same function as you. The world's concepts of
greatness in the human sense mean very little in this
matter of producing a state of peace. I do not care
how insignificant an individual may be; if he finds the
reality of peace in relationship to himself he is making
peace on earth, a state of peace is beginning to appear
on earth. And there is no other way by which it can
appear. There is nothing that anyone can do in the ordinary pattern of struggling with the state of war.
That will never produce peace. It is only when it
begins to appear through the individual, no matter
who he is, where he is, that there begins to be the actual starting point for a state of peace. You may say,
"We've got a long way to go." Yes, it seems that way.
What shall we do? Throw up our hands and say, "Oh!
Useless!"—or are we men and women enough to face
and accept responsibility, real responsibility? That is
the question. And it is that which allows the art of
peace to appear in a world of war, the light to begin to
shine in the darkness; and where the light shines the
darkness has gone, and as the light increases the darkness recedes.

That is the answer, the only practical answer there
is. It points to the key, for the state of peace on earth
will not come through the efforts of human beings on
the basis of their struggling with the state of war. Such
struggles which are going on in the world may have
their value perhaps, in the sense that it is better to be
talking than actually disintegrating one another with
hydrogen bombs. It gives us a little time. But what is
the use of being given a little time if we do not make

use of it? There is only one purpose for such time as we have, and that is to take advantage of the opportunity of making peace, making peace on earth, letting that which we really are come out so that the rightness of our own beings and natures may appear. It is said that you cannot change human nature. Well, perhaps that may be true in a limited sense. We are not really interested in changing human nature. All we are interested in, or should be interested in, is letting our real nature come out—and it will be different to what is called human nature. We will not have had to make human nature over. That just goes by the board when the real nature comes out, just as the darkness goes when the light is turned on.

So, surely, the first concern should be to do whatever is necessary to permit this to come to pass, and we cannot permit it to come to pass as long as we are involved with our struggles with the state of war. As long as that is our first consideration—our own states of turmoil, our own problems and difficulties, our own troubles—we will have them with us for as long as we last. It is only when we begin to give consideration to what is right, and let it find expression through us, regardless of what we think is wrong with somebody else, that we may begin to actually experience the state of peace and learn the art of living in that state. What more wonderful experience could there be, and what greater contribution could anyone, anywhere, give to the world?

God—The Creative Compulsion

"He that overcometh shall inherit all things; and I will be his God, and he shall be my son."

That is the state of providing the facilities by which the creative compulsion works in the affairs of men, and in the affairs of the world.

"But the fearful, and unbelieving, and the abominable, and murderers, and whoremongers, and sorcerers, and idolaters, and all liars, shall have their part in the lake which burneth with fire and brimstone: which is the second death."

That's for them! Reading this list, most people say, "Well, that's about somebody else. I'm not included there." But these descriptive terms point to the fact, not to human fancy (or should I call it subhuman fancy?), the fancy that people have that they couldn't possibly be included in this classification. Yet, who would not be included in the first of these classifications, "the fearful"? And we note that this does head the list. Do you know anyone anywhere in this subhuman scheme of things who is not fearful, who does not yield to fear? One is fearful if one yields to fear. If one is yielding to fear, one is not yielding to the creative compulsion; one is yielding to a control which will destroy.

Now, there are those who say, "Well, you must be afraid; otherwise you will be destroyed. You must be afraid to cross the street; otherwise you won't look both ways." But can't a person look both ways without being afraid? Would it not be the intelligent thing to look both ways? Yet in virtually everything where there is a need to cause people to move, fear is used. There is a great deal of carnage on the highway, as they say. It always amazes me, actually, how little there is when I see these great vehicles roaring through 100 Mile House, tons and tons of lethal object. Yet we go for days without an accident. But because of this carnage, as they call it, it makes people uncomfortable and there is an endeavor to stop it somehow. How? Principally by fear. Show people pictures of the awful accidents that occur, terrible things, so that they will be so afraid of something like that happening to them that they will drive with greater care. The fearful!

One of the most outstanding fields where fear was particularly generated in times past was that of religion. "Be afraid of going to hell!" You may pull up your socks then and graduate to heaven. But the subhuman approach is based in fear. There is this appalling lethargy. No one will do anything unless they are afraid, afraid of losing their job, afraid of whatever it is. This will galvanize them into action sometimes; that on the one hand, and greed on the other. So, being in a subhuman world, we should behave subhumanly; at least this is the general view. And if subhumans won't act the way they should, we'll make them so fearful that they do. But being controlled by fear is destructive. It brings disease, amongst other things. Of course, there are other ways of bringing disease too, but fear is one of them. If you're churning around, fearful inside, you're upsetting your whole endocrine system and something's going to give at the weakest point. How accustomed people are to yielding to fear. It's assumed to be the natural thing to do. But you can't yield to fear and yield to the true creative compulsion at the same time. So, for the most part the creative compulsion is ignored, not even recognized as being present, because people are full up with wrong patterns of yielding.

"The fearful, and unbelieving." How many people are inclined to take the attitude that they'll only believe what they can see. Isn't that a ridiculous attitude? because obviously there is vastly more that you can't see than you can see, and it exists whether you believe in it or not. Yielding to the control of unbelief, a person tries to govern his living—existing it is, not living—on the basis of what he observes. But as he only observes a very small fraction of what is actually there, the decisions he makes are inevitably wrong. Oh, they may seem to be all right for the moment, relative to the things that are very close; but then, you can't make a decision just with respect to one thing, because it always influences other things; like dropping a stone in the water—the ripples go out, and what's going to happen beyond and beyond and beyond is not seen at all. So if there is the endeavor to act on the basis of what the person thinks he sees, he is going to make a mess inevitably. He may, as I say, have an efficient operation close at hand; but when the ripples get out further what's going to happen? What are all the repercussions going to be? How many good things have been done by people, or things that were considered to be good in relationship to what the person saw, that turned out to be terrible things, really. We have noted the population explosion as one thing, simply because people don't know what they're doing. They think they're doing good, mind you, but it multiplies and proliferates problems that they never thought of, and where they had one problem before, which they think they've solved, they have ten more afterwards. So it goes, until there is an overwhelming.

That is why there is a necessity to come up over, overcome, come up higher into a place where there is something which knows what it's doing: this creative compulsion. Becoming aligned with this, then there may be participation in a creative process, in a constructive process, by which not only what is close at hand is handled rightly but the handling rightly of that will have creative repercussions beyond it. So let's not yield to the foolish nonsense of imagining that we can conduct ourselves intelligently on the basis of believing what we see, or believing what we hear. There are quite a few people who conduct themselves on the basis of believing what they hear about this group here. That's their trouble, because it doesn't make any difference to the fact of the matter. But if they try to function on the basis of that limited view they are going to be in trouble one way or another, not because we want to make any trouble for anybody—we don't need to; they make it for themselves.

"And the abominable." Abominable—you know lots of abominable people, I'm sure! But what makes a person abominable? It is the absence of something. It is the absence of love. "The abomination of desolation" is spoken of in another passage in the Bible. Desolation: emptiness, the absence of love, barrenness. It is an abominable state. It is an abomination to the person who has it, and it is abomination to everyone round about. When there is a yielding to resentment, to critical attitudes, to hate, there is an absence of love to that extent, and there is an abominable person. It's true, isn't it? You have experienced being an abomination on occasion, and you've certainly seen others who were abominations. There is no need to judge anyone. You know if there is an abominable state; it's merely the absence of love. And what's needed then? Well, the presence of love, of course. And where is it going

to come from? This creative compulsion. There is a
need for the expression of love. Who's going to express
it? Well, you are, aren't you? If there is an abominable
person, do you have to try to make him more abominable or less abominable? How would you make him less
abominable? Presumably by providing what was absent, which is love. The usual idea is, if a person is
abominable, trample on him. Then you have two
abominable people, because the person who is tram-
pling on the other one obviously has the absence of
love also. So is it every time there is a yielding to any
of these destructive emotions. Now, few people realize
that they are destructive. Some people feel perfectly
justified in resentment: "I resent that; I am justified in
resenting that." Well, you may find justifications for it
but it makes you into an abominable person. Criticiz-
ing, condemning, hating—all these conditions of experience come because there is a yielding to them and a
failure to yield to the creative compulsion.

"And murderers." Oh, none of us are murderers!
How do you know? How do you know that you are
not responsible for having killed somebody? Maybe
you didn't stick a knife in them, or poison them, but
how do you know that some of the repercussions of
what you did on the basis of your mental gymnastics
didn't result in somebody's death? You don't know.
We may be pretty sure that if we have been functioning as subhumans we have been responsible for many
deaths. I think it's a wise precaution that we are not
conscious of the fact; otherwise we couldn't live with
ourselves at all. But if we behave in a subhuman manner because we yield to the wrong things, we are destructive. Whether we believe it or not, whether we
imagine it's true or not, it is so. To be a human being
there must be a yielding to the character, the quality,
of being, not to the things which we come up against

in the environment. Murder. I am sure that we have all been busy murdering ourselves. We succeed in the end, you know, in the subhuman state.

"And whoremongers." Oh, here's one! People sell themselves cheap. If anything in your environment, any other person, any circumstance, can cause you to behave in a manner that does not express and reveal the qualities of the creative compulsion, the qualities of God, in other words, the qualities of being, then you are a whoremonger. You are selling yourself into union with something that should be below you. You are blending with the ill thing with respect to which you are reacting in your environment. You are committing adultery, to put it another way, because we should be blending with the creative compulsion. If we don't do that, we're blending with something else. You can't have a blank state, at least not until you're dead. You're blending with something all the time. There have been those self-righteous people who imagine that they are lily-white in all respects, but if they would just take an honest look at things they would see the truth of the matter, that all are tarred with the same brush, the brush of subhumanity, brought about by the devil of the human mind, the human intellect, which decides that it knows what to do, when it doesn't. It causes people to eat of the fruit of the tree of the knowledge of good and evil. "I know what's good. I know what's going to be good." The person doesn't. He doesn't know what would be good; and the result of eating of that forbidden fruit is what? Death. True. It brings all the tribulations which finally lead to death.

"Sorcerers." Ha, what about that? Did you ever impose anything on anyone else? Did you ever try to make someone behave in a certain way, for their own good of course? That's sorcery, black magic. Of course, black magic includes the control by fear. Anyone who tries to control another person by fear is a sorcerer. Sorcerers are very successful. Witch doctors control by fear, don't they? There are lots of witch doctors across the land, many of them dressed up as medical men, incidentally, trying to control people by fear. Oh, yes! Fear of disease. Why would one have to fight cancer if one was not afraid of it? Why would one have to fight any of these things if one is not afraid of them? Fear. That is no way to clear people from the experience of disease; that's the way to make them diseased. The only way to be cleared from disease is to be one with the creative compulsion of life; in other words to express life. How many medical men do you know who are aware of what it would mean to express life? They know an awful lot about disease; but life and living, what do they know about that? They're just as hopelessly subhuman as everybody else. Now, I am not saying this to condemn the medical profession. You can take any profession, you can take any person, and the same thing applies—subhumanity, the subhuman state which has everything backwards, which consequently goes down instead of up. All the efforts to go up merely make the person go down quicker. That's the way it works, because if one is attuned with the subhuman state one is attuned with that which is moving toward disintegration. Attunement with the creative compulsion moves toward integration. Integration with what? Integration with everything. This is the true ecology, isn't it? Integration with the whole cosmos. That's a powerful operation, you know. So, no sorcery.

"And idolaters." Oh, yes, the country's full of idolaters, and the principal idol is the intellect itself. It can do anything. It can go to the moon. It can solve all problems. All it needs is a few more computers and it gets the job done. So, let's worship the intellect; and if we have some problems (there are a few around), well, they can easily be solved if we educate the intellect a little better. But it is the intellect that has made the problems in the first place; it's going to devise more problems the more it's developed. It is a false god. The mind has its place, but that isn't its place. So, the land is full of idolaters. Of course they worship many other things as well.

"And all liars." Well, anyone who doesn't speak the truth is a liar. And who speaks the truth? How would you speak the truth? By allowing the truth to find expression, which is the creative compulsion. One cannot permit that to occur if the yielding is with respect to all these things round about in the environment, so that we're pushed around by events and circumstances and other people. We're bound to be pushed around by those things as long as we are yielding in that direction. We will find ourselves on the defensive constantly, because someone is going to do something to us we don't like. "I've got to defend myself." If you're on the defensive you're subject to the things against which you are defending yourself. Yield to the creative compulsion. Accept as the most important thing in experience the true quality of the character of being. This can be expressed, this can be revealed, regardless of what's going on in the environment round about. Because the environment tells you to behave a certain way doesn't mean you have to behave that way. You may be compelled by the quality of the true character to express something beautiful and right and effective and powerful into the situation, something that was not a reaction to the situation but was the right action in relationship to that situation. It didn't come from the situation; it came from you. The situation didn't tell you how to behave; you behaved how you should behave on the basis of the true creative compulsion. Then the situation will be caused to change, it will be caused to change in the right way.

The human mind does not know what that right way will be. It can observe it though. But if, seeing the changes coming on this basis, it then looks at the changes and says, "Well, this isn't right. I know better. This isn't good," immediately the individual is yielding to the judgment of the circumstance, the creative compulsion no longer can work, and destructiveness begins all over again.

In this outline there has been portrayed a most excellent revelation of people to themselves. Scarcely anyone reads this verse without thinking of somebody else, certainly not seeing that he himself is involved with every last one of these things, and is going to continue to be so involved as long as the yielding is to the environment, on the basis of the ideas of the mind as to what is good and what is bad. To a subhuman it looks as though there isn't any other way to function. "How else would you do anything? Everything would go all to pieces if I didn't function on this basis." Well, isn't it going to pieces anyway? It is, whether you know it or not. So are you, if you function that way. Why should it be imagined that yielding to the creative compulsion of life would be an impractical experience, when the creative compulsion is capable of operating the cosmos? Is your life such a problem? How quickly the whole world could be changed when there are those who consistently yield to the creative compulsion! It doesn't need very many to let that creative compulsion begin to work in the affairs of men. There is plenty of power; no absence of anything; the presence of everything. Let's let it work.

"He that overcometh shall inherit all things"—all things are added—"and I will be his God," oneness, oneness, "and he shall be my son." Each individual a son or a daughter in the sense of bringing to focus in that person's world this creative compulsion to work in that specific field, something being brought to focus out of the allness of being to the point which the individual is and to work in that person's particular field of responsibility. When it is working so, there is a son or a daughter of God; not the wholeness of God, but a specific focalization, a specific differentiation of being, here on earth. All things belong under the control of this creative compulsion, and if the person lets it be brought to focus in his expression of life all things in the field of his responsibility come under that control; not under the control of the self-active, self-seeking conscious mind, but under the control of that creative compulsion. That is the true dominion. That is the reason for man's existence. If he doesn't fulfil that purpose, there's no point in him existing, so he stops existing. Very natural, isn't it?

Seeing these things, surely we would be willing to yield to the creative compulsion because we are most unwilling to yield to all these other emotional experiences or the concepts of the mind. This creative compulsion is moving in this moment. This is our contact with it, in this moment. It is not as though we could find contact in the future; the future never comes. All we ever have is the moment. It is working now. We can accept it now. We can move with it now.

The Snare of the Fowler

It is a little less than a month to Christmas Day, when this Christian feast is celebrated once again. What a repetitive experience this has been over the centuries! There are two outstanding Christian occasions: one of them is Christmas and the other Easter. By now one would think that people have been sufficiently reminded of what these particular events portray so that no more reminders would be needed; in other words, the actual experience of the truth would be so consistently known in living that there would be no particular point to continuing the celebrations. The fact that these occasions are still celebrated, points to the failure of those who have celebrated them down through the years to let themselves be sufficiently reminded so that they would behave accordingly. These outstanding occasions in the Christian calendar therefore proclaim failure. I don't suppose too many of those who call themselves Christians would agree with my words or would appreciate them; nevertheless they could be true. The opportunity has certainly been provided, for all who would be willing to take advantage of it, to recognize that there is something rightly to be experienced constantly which would obviate being reminded of that twice a year.

Back in the Old Testament, there is a psalm which emphasizes constancy in these words:

"He that dwelleth in the secret place of the most High shall abide under the shadow of the Almighty."

"Dwelling" points to a constant experience. "He that dwelleth in the secret place of the most High." Perhaps this has seemed rather an obscure place, difficult to find. There have been many earnest searchers for that place, indicating thereby that it has been secret, and few there be that find it! The search is usually directed toward some sort of position other than where the individual is. He will go here or he will go there. The going may be a mental excursion or it may even be a physical excursion, maybe to Mecca or Rome. The search has been on in one way or another down through the ages, with the place to be found seen as somewhere other than where the person is. Perhaps we need not imagine that it is simply the physical place where the person is, only, but where the person is both physically and in consciousness. The place is available by reason of the fact that you, for instance, are where you are, physically speaking, and by reason of the fact that you are capable of experiencing something in consciousness. The perennial searcher who seeks truth generally ends up deluding himself, because he constantly imagines that it is somewhere beyond himself. As long as he has this idea, he can never find it. He may spend a lifetime wandering in the wilderness seeking the city to dwell in, and he may enjoy the search, so that his sense of satisfaction is found in the looking. If this occurs, then the person would be disgusted if he found. There are many such. Perhaps they do not have sufficient insight to see it with respect to themselves, but this is the way it is.

The key to the secret place is found in the particular verse which I read: "He that dwelleth in the secret place of the most High." It is because most people are not sufficiently interested in the most high that the place remains secret. Now, when the words, "the most high," are used, these tend to be translated in consciousness as relating to some God high up somewhere, but this is not what is actually said. Reference is not necessarily to the most high God as some would translate it in their own consciousness; just the most high, the most high to you, of course related to what is recognized as being divinely valuable. The most high to some people is simply related to earthly values. Earthly values are not being considered here in the psalm particularly, but what we might call heavenly values. Every person has some, but rather too few pay any attention to them because they become wrapped up in the earthly values, in those things which are supposed to bring ease and comfort in one's own experience. Of course, some imagine that spiritual things may be gained in order to bring this ease and comfort. If that is the attitude, then those are earthly values, not heavenly values. There are, certainly, vast numbers of people who hopefully search here and there—"Lo, here, and lo, there"—seeking in what they suppose are spiritual directions to find ease and comfort for themselves. I suppose this most obviously is confirmed by those who try to use chemical substances of various kinds, either in the form of drugs or alcohol, to produce ease and comfort for themselves. That is following out earthly values. There is nothing heavenly about it whatsoever. Human beings everywhere tend to imagine that their particular brand of earthly values is going to bring the anticipated ease and comfort. Again we have the self-centered state most obviously, the childish state.

The most high relates to those qualities in one's own expression and experience which are of a heavenly nature, not something to be gotten but something to be given. When a person is interested in offering to his fellows and to his world around him the highest of his own expression of love, of understanding, of helpful-

ness, of blessing, of truth, and of life, he begins to
dwell in the place that was before secret when he
wasn't doing that. The self-centered attitude, of
course, always anticipates that the satisfaction is coming from somewhere else to the individual concerned,
"to me," but the true fulfilment comes because the
blessing is given to others. It cannot be sucked into
oneself. It can be breathed out upon others, and whatever it is that is breathed out is what a person knows.
If you have what I believe has been called halitosis,
then your experience is a stinking one, but if the
breath is the sweet breath of heaven, then heaven is
your experience. There is the ease and comfort which
comes, not because you were trying to get it but because you were willing to give something worthwhile
to others, and in that giving the quality becomes
known in your own experience.

"He that dwelleth in the secret place of the most
High." Of course, to the one who dwells there it isn't
secret but is a place in which to abide. In other words,
the release and the expression of the most high is constant. This may remind us of Christmas too, because
the outstanding instruction provided by that occasion
is summarized in the words, "Glory to God in the
highest." People may sing that but seldom see it as
being a practical instruction. What is most high in
your consciousness? The most high always relates to
the true nature of love. We have many, many people
seeking to escape from their particular experience, as
though the circumstances from which they seek to
escape were the cause of their experience. No, that
isn't the cause of anyone's experience. What comes out
of a person in expression, that will either make a person miserable or delighted, that and that alone. We
have people roaming here and there because they
imagine that this circumstance or that circumstance is
displeasing, so one has to move on. Those who are

caught in that trap are lost souls indeed; but nobody made them be lost; that is a state which they chose for themselves. They are empty, valueless, and consequently unhappy. Yet there is available, to the expression of anyone, the most high. The most high is with all people all the time, but if one is blinded by self-seeking, the most high is hidden and the place where the true experience may be known remains secret.

Until one begins to be more keenly aware of the reality of the most high, which is one's own highest vision with respect to the true expression of life in one's own experience, one cannot find oneself; one remains a lost soul. Anyone may dwell in the secret place of the most high, and cause it to become well known, if his concern is with the most high and not with what one is going to get out of it for oneself. What would be the most beautiful thing that could find expression through my lips in this circumstance, the most beautiful action that could appear through my body on this occasion?—this is the approach. What would be most helpful? What would be the highest blessing that I could give? How few there are who ever consider that at all. Most people take the attitude of endeavoring to maneuver things so as to please themselves, and that destroys. What a changed situation immediately appears when a person takes the opportunity of filling his environment with the beauty of his own being, just for the sake of doing that; not for the sake of getting anything out of it but for the sake of the most high, the highest expression of oneself.

Many people think that what have been called, in the dim and distant past, good manners, are for the birds! Fundamentally, good manners should be seen in the light of the expression of what would be a blessing, a thoughtfulness. That brings with it the natural courtesy that is present in the most high. Rudeness is not a part of the quality of the most high, is it? How much we have to give the very moment we consider the most high! That giving is what changes the world.

"He that dwelleth in the secret place of the most High shall abide under the shadow of the Almighty." What is the shadow of the Almighty? Obviously the evidence of the presence of the Almighty. There can be no shadow except there is something present to cast it. When we begin to function on the basis of our own consciousness of the most high, however much that may be at the moment, it causes us to be aligned with the shadow of the Almighty. The spirit of God is the evidence of the presence of God. We become part of the expression of that spirit according to the extent of the release of the most high in our living. We abide under the shadow of the Almighty, of course. Our attitude is very different from what is usual in the experience of human beings.

"I will say of the Lord, He is my refuge and my fortress: my God; in him will I trust."

"Surely . . ."—now here is the absolute certainty consequent upon dwelling in the secret place of the most high, abiding under the shadow of the Almighty consequently. When we do that, we trust God rather than our own self-centered manipulations.

"Surely he shall deliver thee from the snare of the fowler, and from the noisome pestilence."

The fowler, of course, is a person who catches birds. Usually the reason for catching the birds is to make a profit out of it. It is supposed to be a profitable undertaking—and of course one may eat the birds too. The fowler catches birds. Birds portray thoughts. What is it that catches thoughts? Your mind. Some people sometimes claim that terrible thoughts come into their minds. Why? They were snared. The self-centered mind of man is the snare of the fowler. It catches thoughts. There are many, many thoughts wandering around in the atmosphere, and according to the nature of the mental snare, we will catch a particular kind of bird. It isn't by chance that some people are plagued by unpleasant thoughts. How would it be best to place oneself in a position to be plagued by unpleasant thoughts, do you think? By being an unpleasant person! That sort of snare would snare the birds accordingly. We find that we tend to attract the thoughts that relate to our mental condition. The promise is that we might be delivered from the snare of the fowler. When the fifth day of creation came along, the fish and the birds were brought forth, from whence? Were the birds brought forth from out of the air? No, out of the water, as were the fish also. The waters brought forth. In other words, the true process of mental action does not snare birds.

Why is it that the black magician or the witch usually has a raven? Here is the sort of thoughts symbolized. A raven is black, presumably indicating the absence of the Christ spirit, the white spirit. But a raven also exists on dead things, dead flesh. We could say it has a purpose in this regard: it eliminates the offensive decaying substance. If our snare is conducive to ravens, then that's all right: the ravens will eliminate the flesh. We find that such a condition is destructive to the person, but it cleans things up, actually. The true thinking springs forth from the waters; it doesn't come out of the surrounding atmosphere. There are many people who are apparently rather bright, mentally speaking, but who are simply scavengers. Some become really expert in their scavenging. The crow or the magpie will very often pick up bright things and take them away to its nest, imagining that they are of value. Of course they are of utterly no use to a crow, but still it may have a great store of such baubles, and in its crowy consciousness perhaps it thinks of itself as being wealthy. This is what happens to most of the bright snares in the world, those who

think of themselves as being pretty intelligent: they
collect baubles, which are utterly meaningless.

The true process of thinking is not that at all. It
springs forth from the waters. Water symbolizes truth,
doesn't it? There is the essential equipment in man to
permit the expression of what might be called divine
inspiration, divine thinking. It is unknown to those who
are not delivered from the snare of the fowler, those
who have not found what before was the secret place,
the secret place of the most high—the beauty, the
truth, the wonder of being, put first in the assumption
of personal responsibility for letting that be expressed,
letting that be increased on earth, in whatever the circumstance is, wherever the person is, exactly where he
is. If he can't do it where he is, what makes him think
he can do it some place else? Whatever he is doing
where he now is, he will do some place else. If what he
is doing where he is is complaining and rebelling and
getting into a stew about things, he will do that some
place else too; so there is no advantage to going any
place else. When we learn to use the circumstance we
have rightly, fill the world with the beauty which it is
our responsibility to give, then we can also do it any
place else.

How many people in the world are trying to escape
from their circumstances? These are the lost souls,
because the secret place is right exactly where they are.
Why? Because the most high is there, the individual's
consciousness—whatever that may be—of what he or
she may express of beauty, of blessing, of thoughtfulness, of understanding, of helpfulness, of sweetness,
of love, in the circumstance where he is; and that
transforms the circumstance. If no one does that, the
circumstances remain apparently rotten everywhere,
all because of individual personal failure, the failure of
Christians to be Christians. One of the most damning
statements with respect to anyone tends to be, "There

goes such a good Christian person"—there goes someone who maintains the noisome pestilence on earth,
because, you know, good Christians tend to classify
themselves with those who were called Pharisees at
the time of our Master. There were scribes and Pharisees who rejected the truth. They were so righteous in
their own eyes, they were so convinced with respect to
their own beliefs, that they couldn't see the truth right
before them. So it has ever been.

The only way anyone can be delivered from the
snare of the fowler—from self-centeredness; that's it,
isn't it?—and from the results of self-centeredness,
which are described as the noisome pestilence, decay,
is by dwelling in the secret place of the most high.
When someone considers that possibility they are inclined to wonder as to what they are going to lose.
Well, of course, if a person approaches things in that
way, obviously he is proclaiming—placard back and
front—"I am self-centered," and if you are self-
centered you are part of the noisome pestilence, a pestilence on earth. Human beings have become pests,
haven't they? We think of pests as being a swarm of lo-
custs, or something of this nature, which clean off all
the green growth in their path. That's just about what
human beings do, isn't it? Destruction wastes at noon-
day because of human beings.

Yet, the secret place of the most high is here. The
kingdom of heaven is at hand for anyone who takes
the trouble to lift up his eyes to the most high, with
the sole concern of giving glory to the most high in the
highest way possible to the individual himself. That
may vary from individual to individual, but each one
can do it according to his highest awareness of what
this would be; and that begins to fill the world with
beauty. There begins to be the experience of the reality of home. Some people imagine that home is a place
to escape into or to escape from. It is neither. It is a

place in which to dwell because the most high comes first in one's attitude, in one's practice, in one's doing, in one's speaking, in one's thinking—indeed, yes, in your thinking. What birds are snared by you? Oh, there are flocks of crows and magpies, carrion-loving birds, to be snared; and people everywhere are snaring them all the time, even though the birds they catch tear their own flesh. But there is the creative process by which the life forms at all levels of consciousness are brought forth, not from the self-centered world around us but from the waters, the truth, according to the divine design under control. The birth takes place in the mental equipment and there rise up through all levels of consciousness the beautiful living forms which reveal the wonder of God's love on earth, symbolized by the fish of the sea and the birds of the air. The fish are given into the sea, the birds are given into the air. Because of this there is the delight of living, the evidence of home, the shadow of the Almighty.

Yes, children need to learn. Some say that Christmas is for children. If it has any meaning, that's about it, I guess. Children need to learn, but mature people should know, should dwell in, the secret place of the most high which is no longer secret, abide under the shadow of the Almighty, safely home, trusting God. Then there is deliverance, and as we are delivered the reason for the necessity of deliverance becomes very plain to us. It's not particularly plain before we are delivered, but we know it when we are. So we may, if we will, in this moment and in every moment, dwell, abide, live, constantly experience, the most high in expression through us in the place where we are.

The Worth of Work

This day falls in the Labor Day weekend, a day set apart to honor the working people. I think what really needs to be honored is work itself. There needs to be a true valuation of its worth. What is the value of work? Is it what is paid to a person for doing it? Is that what gives value to work? Apparently most imagine that it is. There is always concern for such pay, plus fringe benefits, as may be forthcoming. A good job is a job which pays plenty. But is it really what a person gets because of his work that gives the work value, or gives the person value? We have recognized that a rather different approach is required, for it is actually what a person puts into his work that causes the work to be of value and reveals the value of the person. We devaluate ourselves if we imagine that the value of the work we do is what comes out of it. Work has value if a person has value in the doing of that work. All true values are consequent upon people, consequent upon the amount of the individual value that is put into whatever is done. If a person values himself very little and consequently does not consider it worthwhile to put much into what he is doing, what he is doing will have precious little value. What we put into what we do gives what we do value, and in the doing of it we have an increased sense of our own value.

This is something that is so largely lacking in the

experience of people everywhere. There is this sense
of discontent, constant discontent. No matter how
much comes out of a job in the way of pay or fringe
benefits or what-have-you, it doesn't allay this sense of
discontent. Momentarily, if there is a raise in pay everybody is happy, but almost immediately it wasn't
quite enough! Particularly in these bargaining sessions
that they hold, it never is what was originally asked
for. Of course, perhaps the individual didn't quite expect to get that, but it leaves a sense of discontent
when it is not received. There is this underlying discontent everywhere because value is being placed in
the wrong things. Unless we are aware of our own
value we will naturally be discontented. If we try to
convince ourselves of our own value by what we get
out of what we do, we will never find a state of contentment, because the value is in us and not in the
work as such. The work has value, or is given value,
because of us, because of the individual himself. If the
individual doesn't have value, no matter what he does
it will not have value. So the concern is to have a correct valuation of oneself, and one will begin to have
a correct valuation in this regard as there is an increased experience of the value he puts into whatever
he does. If you put value into something it comes from
you; because it comes from you, you have an awareness of it; and because you have an awareness of it
you have a consciousness of your own worth. If you
don't put anything into the job, but expect to have a
sense of value by reason of what you get out of it, you
will be empty, discontented. We see this state of affairs everywhere because human beings have placed
their values where they do not belong, really. If we
are anything, if we are worth anything, then what we
do has value because we put ourselves into it. It is our
worth that we put into what we do, and that gives
what we do value. What comes out of it from the

standpoint of benefit to us is beside the point. Something will come out of it but we do not rightly work for that reward.

We might note something that our Master emphasized at one point: "Do not your alms before men, to be seen of them. . . ." If you do, if you make a big splash and say, "I am worth more than I am getting; I must have more," then you have your reward. Maybe you get fired, I don't know, but you may get more. In either case you have your reward; but you don't feel your own value; it doesn't cause you to have a consciousness of your own value. Of course, human beings have been putting worth where it doesn't belong for so long, they imagine that if they are getting a high rate of pay that must mean they are of value. But it doesn't, necessarily, at all, and the individual knows it inside, and that's why he's discontented. But he keeps following the carrot in front of his nose and tries to give himself a sense of value by getting more from what he does. But that is not what gives a sense of value. We don't need to get a sense of value, because we have value. But we have not had an adequate consciousness of our own value, and we only begin to have an adequate consciousness of our own value when we give value, not when we get it. When we get it it may build our egos, we may be able to put on a good front, but inside we feel just the same—more or less worthless.

And yet there is an inherent awareness that we must have some sort of value. Let's find out what it is. We can't find out what it is without putting into what we do the value which we have. To the extent that we do this, do what we do wholeheartedly, we begin to discover our own value; we begin to be aware of our own worth. Why? Because we have expressed it. Our value relates to spirit, the nature of our spirit. Spirit is the causative factor with respect to that which appears in form. Our concern is with right spirit, doing what we do with our whole hearts. Now this requires that we put into it such capacity as we have. We can't ignore any of our capacities and have a sense of value. There was a parable, wasn't there, about the talents. Some put them to work and experienced a sense of value in consequence. One person thought he didn't have very much; he buried it in the ground. He had no sense of worth, no sense of value. It isn't whether we judge that our capacities are small or great that matters; but what do we give into what we do, of what we have, of what we are?

It is vitally important that one should have respect for oneself, and this includes a consciousness of one's own value, not in a conceited sense—this is a front, this is a bubble which gets pricked by and by—but a sense of real worth because we put something real into what we do. And this, bringing a sense of content, also brings joy in living. Because we do this doesn't mean that we don't receive what is coming to us. We always receive what is coming to us, one way or another. Some people think they have more coming to them than they are getting, in the sense that what they should be getting is more money. They may manage to get more money by various means, but with it they get a lot of other things too that they were not too anxious to get. But once there is this involvement in the processes of getting, in order to experience increased value in relationship to oneself, one is going to be getting a lot of things that weren't bargained for. And this is something that most people fail to appreciate. Then, of course, there apparently is reason for more complaint.

The answer is not in the getting but in the giving, in what we offer into what we do—I don't care what it is that we do. What do you offer when you speak to somebody else? What is it that you offer into your task of the moment? Do you offer something that is of value? Or, in speaking to someone, do you take value away? In doing what you do, do you give value into what you are doing, or do you subtract value? If something is done in an attitude of boredom, if something is done in an attitude of rebellion, if something is done in an attitude of resentment, you are taking something away; you are not adding anything; you are not increasing value. If something is done with joy, if something is done because you love to do it, if something is done to express effectiveness, then something is given, something is added, something is increased, value is expressed. And because you express value you become aware of the value which you have expressed; you become aware that this value came from you; that you, therefore, have value. And while this may not all be thought out in the mind, it is what the experience is. If you offer something in conversation that criticizes or condemns or complains or resents, you are not offering anything of value. You are offering something which, to the degree that others respond to it and are affected by it, decreases value; therefore you have a lesser sense of value in relationship to yourself.

We determine our own experience of value, and we will find that when we express true value it correlates with the values in our environment; in other words, the value in the outer sense takes form. We don't have to get a reward. Whatever is needful comes to us, not because we are trying to get it, not necessarily because it comes from the place that we expect it. And this is something that needs to be recognized, because people are always insisting that if they are going to get something it has to come in a certain way, on a certain basis, at a certain time. I think all the labor contracts that are drawn up nowadays are an indication of this. There is no trust, there is no awareness, that if one is right oneself the right effect will appear. There is no trust in this. Nobody really believes it. You have to fight for everything you're going to get! And it seems this way to human beings because this is what they have decided to do. They are going to fight for everything they are going to get and they are going to make sure they are going to get it thus and so. It's all supposed to be a foregone conclusion; everybody's going to be satisfied. But are they? Oh, no! They may get the things they bargain for, in that sense, but they get a lot of other things they didn't bargain for, because they had set the cycle in motion by reason of this insistence upon trying to get, rather than offering the thing of value.

Trusting the value: this is trusting God. Trusting God is usually rather a vague thing in human consciousness, but it is trusting the thing that is of real value. It could be said that it is trusting yourself, trusting the value that you are, expressing that value and letting it go at that—just expressing that value and not saying, "Well, now, I've got to see where the reward is coming from." If you have that attitude you are denying your own value. It is only as the value is expressed, without strings, that the true value comes in return. And the true value is not necessarily the value that the individual had decided should be the reward. You may put something into some task that from the human standpoint looks as though "there's no reward going to come out of this!" You're not looking for a reward. You are expressing your value. This is what brings delight in life, to express one's own value without thought of reward. Something will come back, but it may not come back from that particular task. It may come back from somewhere totally different, totally seemingly unrelated. It will come back, though—not that we are concerned about that; we just note it in passing. We are taken care of; everything's under control.

No matter how much human beings try to set up their patterns of receiving, getting, to make sure that they are going to be "well covered" in every direction, they never are. It never is satisfying. It never provides what is needful. The individual doesn't feel the truth of himself. He becomes the plaything, almost, one might say, of all these external forces that he's bargained for—they are going to run his life henceforth. Red tape is included in that, isn't it? It requires a vast bureaucracy to provide everything for everybody, but it leaves out the one thing that is necessary. So far, apparently, most people have not seen this. They must get better conditions of some kind; they must get more money; they must get this, they must get that; and when they have all these things, then they'll be satisfied. But the more people get, the less satisfied they are, because they are ignoring the thing that brings contentment. It isn't the getting; it's the awareness of one's own worth, the awareness that one has value, the awareness of respect for oneself and that one does not need to be propped up by all these things round about. The more we are propped up, the more conscious we become of our own weakness, of our own inadequacy—"We have to have all these things to make us worth anything." But it's not so! These things do *not* make us worth something. They detract from our worth, because they insist that we maintain a false belief, a false outlook, a false view of things. Our value is in what we are, regardless of all these things. We're worth something anyway, and it is this worth that we need to experience.

Recently some of us were reading from a book about Africa. The lady who wrote it recognized what she called "the hole in the heart," the emptiness in the hearts of the African people in general because this vital factor, of which I am speaking now, has been ignored. It is always supposed that the "benefits of civili-

zation," so called, are going to make people happy.
Oh, no! certainly not! Contentment does not come that
way. It comes because we express our own value. And
if people are made to think that they are going to feel
valuable, feel worthwhile, feel content, because they
are piled high with all this stuff of civilization, they
are functioning on a basis of complete self-delusion. It
does not work that way. Now, when I say that, I am
not saying there is necessarily anything wrong with
these things, but these things are made to be wrong by
human beings in their attitudes toward them. It's not
the things themselves that are wrong; it's human beings that are wrong.

Only when we begin to see that we have value already, even though we have not experienced it adequately yet, do we have a right starting point, because
we begin to give what we have of our own value into
what we do. We do this freely, without reservation.
We're not holding back. We're not holding back because someone's not going to pay us enough for it. We
give what we are because it's our nature to do it. This
is our nature, and if we deny this nature we are very
discontented people; we are unhappy, disturbed. Do
we see any of this sort of experience in human lives
anywhere? Of course we do. We see it everywhere,
simply because there is a failure to see the truth of the
matter, because values have been placed where they
don't belong. Human beings feel less and less respect
for themselves by reason of all these things that are
conceived to be necessary to make the human being of
value, make him worth something. He has no value of
himself, apparently. He has to have all these things to
make him worth something. If one has such an approach, then he is going to feel empty inside. There's
going to be a hole in the heart, a hole in the heart
based upon something that is a lie but nevertheless
it's the experience.

We have value. But how are we going to find out that we have value? By giving the value that we have into what we do—everything. Sometimes a person will say, "Well, I am not going to give very much to that person; he won't appreciate it." Then there are people who imagine that they have been giving to their children, perhaps. Then the children grow up and don't pay any attention to them. "After all I've given, this is my reward." Well, evidently the individual didn't give, if that is his attitude. If you give something to someone, you are not looking for a reward.

It is your true nature to give something that is of value into the environment to others, in your thinking, in your feeling, in your acting. These are the channels of giving. What is the spirit that is expressed through these channels? What is it that is being given? Is it of value? If it is of value you will have an increasing sense of your own worth, of your own meaning, and the hole in the heart begins to be filled up. If you are always looking for someone else to provide something for you so that you may feel happy, so that you may feel contented, you will never feel happy or contented. You may have a momentary experience which you interpret that way, but only a momentary one; and it isn't real happiness; it isn't contentment. You can't know that without knowing yourself, and you can't know yourself without expressing yourself—expressing your own true value.

So work, labor, is most useful. It's a wonderful thing because here is the opportunity to express your value. If there is a state where there is nothing to do—and I really can't imagine such a state; some people claim that they have nothing to do, but that is usually because they are trying to get something; there's nothing to get, they think—but if it were possible to be in a state where there was nothing to do, you would have no means to experience your own sense of value.

When people get trapped with the idea that there is nothing to do they get bored; they have no sense of their own value. People do get bored, of course, and it seems like a terrible affliction. They imagine that because in some certain circumstance there is nothing more to get, nothing more to get out of it, therefore they must be bored. But how about considering the possibility that there's something to give into it? How about considering the possibility that one has sufficient value oneself that one can give into the situation and cause that to be valuable, whatever it is? There is always something that can be done. As long as you're alive you can always breathe. You can always breathe out a breath. So let us see where the real value is. The real value is in oneself, in the divine sense. You have something divine to give, to offer, to increase value in the environment.

Consider this biblical passage:

"Then the Lord answered Job out of the whirlwind, and said,

"Who is this that darkeneth counsel by words without knowledge?

"Gird up now thy loins like a man; for I will demand of thee, and answer thou me.

"Where wast thou when I laid the foundations of the earth? declare, if thou hast understanding.

"Who hath laid the measures thereof, if thou knowest? or who hath stretched the line upon it?

"Whereupon are the foundations thereof fastened? or who laid the corner stone thereof;

"When the morning stars sang together, and all the sons of God shouted for joy?"

Here is a most wonderful portrayal of true living, the creative expression of life. Why is it that human beings don't know about these things? Because they have not girded up their loins like men and women. They have been intent upon trying to get for themselves. What are they going to give? What are they going to express into life? It is in the giving that the knowing comes, the knowing of one's own true value, the increased knowing of why one is giving, what the purpose is. You can't know that without doing it. You can't know ahead of time. You can't figure it out. Human beings have been trying to figure these things out and have made theories of all kinds about it, but none of these theories are really true, none of them. Nobody knows. Nobody knows until they do it, until they let the value which is inherent in themselves be expressed in their own actions, in their own living, into their own environment, that the environment may be filled with value. If it is imagined that the environment is already full of value and you can get it out of there, you are going to run out of value one of these days; there won't be any more left. This is what is happening in the world, isn't it? There's going to be an almighty bust one of these days! because human beings are trying to get value out of everything, get it while the getting's good because pretty soon there won't be any more value left to get—and then what?

We begin to discover that our purpose is to give value, not to get it—to give value—and it is in the giving, in the expression of it, because in what we are thinking and feeling and saying and doing we are increasing value, the real values, that we begin to experience delight in living. "When the morning stars sang together, and all the sons of God shouted for joy." Here is what happens. Here is happiness, one might say; here is fulfilment; here is everything. What do we have to give? What values do we have to express? These are the true values, and when we express them, then the things round about take on value; they reflect the true values. But if the true values aren't there, there is nothing to be reflected and we struggle around in the pit of false values, laboring so hard and being so miserable. Our Master spoke of those who labored and were heavy laden. Poor people! Most people view this as indicating that our Master sympathized with this terrible state. Nonsense! He was showing that it was completely unnecessary to be in that sort of state. While He didn't come out and say it, He might have said, "Why are you so stupid, to stay that way?" "Come unto me, all ye that labour and are heavy laden"—all you who are in that miserable state—"come unto me, come out of it, start to live, start to give expression to the true values. Take my yoke upon you, and learn of me. . . ." Well, why not do it? Why not do it? We have every opportunity in the world. The more opportunity we have to work—and who doesn't have that opportunity?—the more we are able to give, the more value we are able to express, the more value begins to be placed in the environment because we put it there, not because we took it away. And we will find that all necessary to the fulfilment of life, in the external sense, is added; it's there. We don't have to worry about it. It's increasing, after all, if we're putting more value into the environment.

So may we share in the creative fulfilment of life. So may we be in place, and we, being in place, can answer the question: "Where wast thou?" or "Where art thou?" Remember the question the Lord asked of Elijah: "What doest thou here, Elijah?"—"What are you doing in that miserable mess?" And that question is being asked of mankind: "What are you doing in this awful state?" There's no need to be there. We can come out of it any time we choose, when we start to allow our own true value to be given on earth.

The Authority of Doing

Contained in the 5th, 6th and 7th chapters of the Gospel according to Matthew is what has been called the Sermon on the Mount. It has been generally assumed, I think, that these words were spoken to the multitudes by Jesus, who stood on high ground to do it. The words themselves are perhaps looked upon as a sermon, as though they had all been spoken on this one occasion. I do not think that this is a very accurate picture. First of all, nowhere does it say that He spoke to the multitudes. He spoke to His disciples. He may have stood on, or sat on, high ground to do it, but even that wasn't really the point. He spoke to them from a higher level of consciousness. The words as they appear in these three chapters were likely simply a summary of what He said on many occasions at greater length. It seems to be imagined by some that Jesus never really said anything that wasn't recorded in the Bible. If so, He must have been silent for most of the time.

At the beginning of the 5th chapter of Matthew these words are recorded in the first two verses:

"And seeing the multitudes, he went up into a mountain: and when he was set, his disciples came unto him:

"And he opened his mouth, and taught them, saying. . . ."

He spoke to His disciples; He spoke to those who had a certain openness of response to Him. These are the ones that He taught, whether on this particular occasion or some other. It is impossible to teach anyone who is not open to receive what is taught. Many schoolteachers have discovered this. There must be response if there is to be teaching.

In connection with these things of which our Master spoke, these words are recorded toward the end of the 7th chapter:

"Therefore whosoever heareth these sayings of mine, and doeth them, I will liken him unto a wise man, which built his house upon a rock:

"And the rain descended, and the floods came, and the winds blew, and beat upon that house; and it fell not: for it was founded upon a rock.

"And every one that heareth these sayings of mine, and doeth them not, shall be likened unto a foolish man, which built his house upon the sand:

"And the rain descended, and the floods came, and the winds blew, and beat upon that house; and it fell: and great was the fall of it."

You will note that the distinction between these two groups of people—those who built their house upon the rock, and those who built their house upon the sand—was not in the hearing. Both groups heard. The difference was in the doing; it required doing. This particular passage concludes the words that are supposedly included in the Sermon on the Mount. Then there are the last two verses of the 7th chapter:

"And it came to pass, when Jesus had ended these sayings, the people were astonished at his doctrine:

"For he taught them as one having authority, and not as the scribes."

There was something about the way He spoke that impressed people. In an endeavor to define the distinction, these particular words were used: "He spoke as one having authority, and not as the scribes." He had just finished indicating the importance of doing. He had been saying something, and what He said was evidently the evidence of His doing, therefore carrying authority. Very many people, when they wish to give authority to their words, quote someone else. This has been done continuously within the range of what has been called Christianity. The minister would point to what Jesus said.

One of the characteristics that was emphasized in our Master's ministry was that He did use scripture, but then very often He would follow this up with the words, "But *I* say unto you. . . ." And what He said was founded in no other authority than what He was. When someone is teaching someone else something, comment may be made, "Do as I say, not as I do." Such words, of course, carry no authority. It is the fact of doing that gives words authority. It was because of the doing of Jesus that He could say something, so that what He said was based upon what He did. Most people seem to want to say first and do later—if they do at all.

I wonder how many words would be spoken if all our speaking was based upon our doing. I am thinking of this from the standpoint of right speaking. Of course the fact of the matter is that no matter what we do we teach by what we do; it is our doing that teaches others. Some may hear the teaching and follow it, some may ignore it, but whatever anyone does, it is offered as an example to somebody else, obviously so. We may presumably imagine that we can do certain things in secret, so to speak. The thought may be hidden, even the action may be hidden, so that we assume that what we do therefore is not what we are teaching. But what we do is what we are; it is a revelation of what we are; and therefore what we are goes around with us and it is constantly impinging upon others. There is a constant influence present.

Influences are not always consciously recognized. Very much of our experience in living is consequent upon subconscious influences. We do many things which are the evidence of such influences, and these influences stem from the doing, from the experience, of others who are now present in the world, or through others who have passed from this sphere of things but whose influence comes down to us through heredity. Our doing, then, is a rather composite affair which influences those in our immediate vicinity, and we find ourselves, consciously or unconsciously, being influenced by the doing of others. If all this doing is faulty, is a mixed-up state, then the interchanging influences merely add to the confusion. Obviously there is need for some sort of doing to appear on earth which is not based in this mixed-up condition. Our Master was pointing to this in what He said in the Sermon on the Mount. "Here is the truth of right doing," He was saying. "Here is the truth that I exemplify before you because I am not subject to all these mixed-up influences of the doings in the world." He spoke as one having authority because He had authority, based in His own doing and His own consequent example.

Now He didn't speak to the multitudes. He didn't teach, or endeavor to teach, those who were not open in their response to Him. On various occasions during the course of His ministry there were those who took issue with Him; there were those who sought to engender some sort of a conflict, to put Him in the wrong somehow. In other words, there were those who were opposed to Him and whose opposition occasionally became vocal. We may note that opposition is a form of response, so on each occasion He dealt with it, because whether the individuals realized it or not they were offering Him response; probably not the kind He would have preferred but He used it to advantage nevertheless and, in fact, He taught through it. Probably He didn't teach those who opposed Him but He did teach those who were open to Him and were present on the occasion. He taught by His doing, and of course His words emphasized what He was doing.

The only ones He did not teach, or the only people who were not capable of playing any part in His ministry, were those who were indifferent. They came and went. They may have heard some words but they didn't understand; they weren't interested. They didn't feel that what He was saying meant anything to them. Why not? Because as yet they were too self-centered; they were too wrapped up in themselves. They were so involved with themselves that they couldn't even summon up enough energy to oppose, let alone respond. And there are many such in the world today. But by reason of circumstances it becomes more difficult to balance on the fence. People are dropping off, on one side or the other.

So there are these three categories: the hot and the cold and the lukewarm. The statement was, "I would thou wert cold or hot." From the standpoint of achievement it doesn't matter which, because both provide response. The coldness, or the opposition, is of no blessing to those who are cold and oppose, but what happens does assist the outworking of the true purpose on earth. People inadvertently assist this creative unfoldment by opposing. Of course the joyous thing, the satisfying thing, the fulfilling thing, appears by reason of those who are open in their response, who love the truth exemplified on earth. Until the truth is exemplified on earth, all that people can love is their particular idea or concept or belief about the truth, because the truth remains invisible and to that extent incomprehensible. It is only as the truth emerges into form that people can understand it. Only those people who respond can actually understand it. Those who oppose certainly don't understand it but they are affected by it. Those who are indifferent don't understand it and they remain in their vegetable condition until finally, if they do not respond or oppose, they will get spued out anyway. If you lie in the gutter you must expect to go down the drain.

What is required on earth is something that carries authority, but not the authority of the scribes. We have many preachers, some very prominent preachers, who use as a basis for their considerations, "The Bible says. . . ." The Bible says. The question really is, What is the person who speaks actually saying? "The Bible says, but what do I say?" This should be the approach of anyone. The Bible certainly provides some wonderful guides for people to move in the right direction. We also have the words of Jesus, specifically, one who taught with authority and not as the scribes. But He suggested that only those who not only said, but did, would build a house immovable upon the rock. It isn't a matter of saying, "The Bible says"; it is a matter of doing something, and the doing rightly precedes the saying. One is on sinking sand if one tries to say, from the standpoint of what one imagines the truth to be, before one has done it. The saying carries authority by reason of the doing.

Most people find themselves in the position where they are subject to the sayings and the doings—the example—of other people, present and past. We have group categories in this regard, what we might call false dualities, very often. A person's doing, the evidence of what he is in this sense, will be based in the particular category into which he falls. The doing, for instance, is supposed to be one thing in the "establishment," whatever that means, and another thing in the —what would it be?—nonestablishment. But here is conformity to what others are doing, subjection to the influence which is extended by what others do. Sometimes that doing is related to high-sounding saying which has very little to do with the doing; in other words, everyone tends to try to explain away the nature of his doing by his saying. And we have some very effective words spoken, which influence a lot of people, that certainly do not indicate any basis in the fact of doing. We have a lot of people who talk about love and peace but, for instance, whose doing may end up in a riot. The doing and the saying have very little connection. Certainly the world would be a much quieter place if all saying were based in right doing. Then there would be something that really carried some authority. But how easily people are swayed by what others say, even though they don't do it.

We have a number of dual classifications in the world, as I have mentioned. We have East and West. Presumably this relates to what is called the communist and non-communist world. That's rather a backhanded thing, isn't it? What's a non-communist? What is he? Just not a communist? What would that be? There needs to be something. Perhaps the successes of communism may be attributed to the fact that they think of themselves as being something, whereas those who are not communists apparently don't think of themselves as being anything; they're just simply non-communist. So there are these contending classifications of people. But what is being conveyed by any classification of people is on the basis of the doing, really, and not on the basis of what is said.

It is perhaps this apparent hypocrisy that has disturbed young people of every generation. This is supposed to be some sort of modern phenomenon, but it happened in every generation. There are more young people nowadays, that's all, and there is more noise therefore, and more effect. But the mere recognition

that there is hypocrisy in the so-called establishment
has achieved very little, if that's all it is, because immediately there begins to be an equally hypocritical
state into which those who criticize the other state fall.
We have these contending factions—I suppose young
and old, in the larger picture—and each establishment
sees something wrong with the other. How much energy is given to decrying the wrong things that are present in the other establishment! And we find this sort
of condition in everything of man's experience on
earth. We have political parties who indulge in the
same sort of contention. In this country the Democrats
see the devil in the Republicans, and the Republicans
in the Democrats. Then sometimes there are those
who change their allegiance, so that the devil swaps
places. But all this is in the realm of what might be
called the scribes—people who back up their stands
on the basis of what someone else said or did, or tradition, or lack of tradition, or something. And the true
authority goes by default.

The true authority emerges because there is a true
authority. That true authority is vaguely recognized
by mankind, perhaps more particularly by those who
are interested in the scientific world in all its various
ramifications. There is a recognition of authority there.
Things behave the way they behave. There is a pattern. There is a design. There is the rule of law, one
might say. There is order. There is authority. Somehow this authority sticks. Human beings have tried in
various ways, for their own advantage presumably, to
break that authority. "It would be very convenient,"
some have thought, "if we could break the authority of
the rule of gravity; then we could go flitting around."
Of course, the idea is just to break it for oneself, not
for anybody else, because if you broke it for everybody, then we all go flying off into space. But some-

how or other the true establishment makes its laws stick, and we can't violate them with impunity.

So there is an authority at work already, present within the range of human experience. Yet everybody tries to set up authority on the basis of human concept and idea and desire, disregarding the authority that is already established, particularly if it interferes with what we want to do. So we have this confused state of behavior on earth which produces, inevitably, conflict. There must be conflict until the true authority begins to operate within the range of human experience in right doing. Then, having accepted this as the most important thing, so that we do something, we may, as needed, talk about it, and what is then said carries the authority of the doing. But woe to those who talk with respect to spheres of function in which they have no experience.

Let us be clear that this doesn't mean we have to have experience of all the distorted states that are present in the world of man. Who wants to talk about those things anyway? Apparently a lot of people! For instance, we have the perennial question nowadays of so-called drug abuse, and everybody wants to talk about it. What's the point? What's the point of talking about it? Those who indulge in such things may be said to have the authority to talk about it, but they're the ones who are in trouble—and that includes virtually the whole population, incidentally. There are all kinds of drugs, you know. I wonder where that term "drug abuse" came from. How do you abuse a drug? People abuse themselves. They abuse themselves by using drugs of all kinds. So we have the idea, very prevalent, that it is important to talk about the distorted things there are in the world, that somehow if we talk enough about these things they will go away. The more we talk about them the more we have them, and the more people will be doing, so that they know what they're talking about. But is there any advantage to knowing what one is talking about with respect to something which is a complete distortion? to something which is self-abuse? And there is a wide range of consideration open to human beings in this regard, because they've been abusing themselves for centuries.

So we have a vast history to examine as to all the methods of human self-abuse, and we can talk about it for years. We can study it, we can write books about it, we can multiply information about it, but to what end? What's going to be achieved by it? What's supposed to happen? Is it going to go away? Is it going to stop? Are people going to be any better for all their talk and all their study? What futility! What utter confusion! What chaotic nonsense! Yet people grow up generation after generation and go right into that sort of pattern. And, you know, young people grow old; they've done it every generation. And then the young person is an old person. There's a new generation of young people—"Oh, you old fogies!" But it's the same old thing over and over and over again.

People may know something about the truth, for instance, but that's not what they do. They do something entirely false and then they discuss it. Isn't that most of the conversation in the world?—gossip, for one thing. But people do all kinds of crazy, nonsensical things and then spend their lives discussing it, as though something of value is going to emerge out of all that. But it's been done generation after generation, and in this sense there is nothing new under the sun. There is something new *in* the sun. How about building your house upon the rock, for a change?

We have some sayings, we have some teachings. According to our response, in the measure that we are disciples, we hear these things. And then the question arises as to whether we are interested in doing them or not, or whether we are more interested in discussing, and therefore hearing, those things which are of the distorted pattern. There seems to be some sort of fatal fascination about the widespread state of distortion there is in the world, and people want to know all about it. "Tell me about it." And there is literature without end about all this—absolutely valueless. Of course people in the world the way it is study this carefully and store it away and have all this information. They get letters after their names for doing this, and it's supposed to be important. But the world remains a mess, and it gets a worse mess all the time, because certainly attention is being paid to all the wrong things. It is admitted that they are the wrong things, because the idea is supposedly that we're going to solve these knotty problems. Do you really believe that? My, oh my, people are surely deluded!

Where there is a beginning response to the truth the individual will hear the saying. He is open to hear, to some degree anyway. Usually the hearing is conditional, to start with. If he likes what he hears he'll listen some more. If it doesn't conform with what he wants to hear, then very often response closes off and he stops hearing. But there are those, thank God, who, even though they don't like some of the things they hear, are willing to go on hearing. That's a start. If nobody will listen, there's no starting point. But the starting point doesn't amount to anything until there begins to be some doing. That's why things collapsed at the time of Jesus, because there was so little doing. There was hearing; quite a few heard. But most people hear in order to discuss, in order to argue, so that they may avoid discovering what the truth really is—because the truth can never be found by discussion; it can never be known by argument. This is an area where human beings have applied methods to prevent themselves from ever coming to know the truth. Dis-

cussion, argument, study—all this means nothing until
a person knows the truth. Then there may be some
value, but the value is in a different way. It isn't to
find out the truth but to see how it may best operate
in the various fields of responsibility.

We never find out the truth by discussing what is
false. We never discover the truth by arguing about
distortions, and we never know the truth by taking the
attitude, "Well, I know a very great deal about distortions." We may be ever so wise in that regard, and
ever so stupid when it comes to knowing the truth.
The truth becomes known to those who not only hear
but do, not only understand something of the right
way to go but go in that right way. Isn't it strange that
it seems to take quite exceptional people to do it? This
is a very, very rare experience on earth. Cover everything up, is the usual approach, with a flood of words.
But to do—this is the only thing that has meaning. It
was the fact of our Master's doing, the truth of what
He was in action, that caused His words to carry authority. He said, "You know what the scripture says
but evidently you don't know what it means, because
you do not have the experience of it. This is the way it
is. I am the example. My words, therefore, are the
truth. Hear me." All right, some have been inclined to
admit the possibility of that insofar as Jesus was concerned, but what about us? How is it for us? What are
we? How do we behave? What do we do? Do we still
have the futile imagination that we have to do all the
wrong things in order to discover the right things? in
other words, to indulge ourselves in self-centeredness
in order to become God-centered? Isn't that rather
foolish? Yet this is the way people behave.

It may be that there is a time when there is a working through self-centeredness, but for heaven's sake,
let's emerge out of it on the other side! Let us come
clear of involvement in this self-centered approach, so

that hearing the truth we may align ourselves with the truth and grow up. That permits us to mature. To stay in the self-centered condition is to remain childish.

The words that are spoken on earth carry authority when there are those whose lives reveal the doing. And this is an exceptional thing in the world of man. Only those will begin to be affected by it who are open in response one way or another, either in yielded response because at last they hear something that strikes a chord in their own hearts and they know that, however painful the idea may be to them at the moment, nevertheless it's just what they have been looking for—here are the ones who are affected in the way that leads them to the experience of the truth for themselves—or there are, of course, those others who are affected adversely because they oppose. They are responding too, by opposition, and there is no blessing to them in that, unless they get hurt sufficiently so as to awaken to the right sort of response. So the authority of God affects those who respond. For the moment it doesn't affect the indifferent, but, as I have indicated, it is becoming progressively more difficult for people to remain indifferent. The day will come when it's impossible.

Let us accept the responsibility ourselves for speaking with authority. That carries some strings, doesn't it? It carries the strings of doing the right thing, of being the right thing, of revealing the truth. Then whatever is spoken carries the authority of the truth. Those who respond will sense the authority, either by yielding or by opposing. And that authority is absolute, just as absolute as gravity. Let us play our part in letting it appear on earth, that the way of salvation may be present with the children of men and they may not be fooled into imagining that their arguments and their conflicts between different classifications are the way to salvation. This is what human beings have imagined for a long time. It never was true, but there has so seldom been anything on earth that could reveal the fact that it wasn't true. Our Master did, but He wasn't on earth long. And here we are, with the opportunity to let it be so now, that what finds expression through us out of the abundance of our hearts may carry the true authority.

Unashamed to Praise the Lord

How very beautiful is a song offered in praise to the Lord. It seems that these days most human beings are ashamed to praise the Lord. In times past most of the music, art and architecture was designed to give glory to God. People were delighted to do this. Of course, the thought of giving glory to God tended originally to be based in the idea of propitiating God. In other words, the approach was basically a self-centered one. The endeavor was to have God provide what human beings deemed to be necessary to themselves for their pleasure and success. So the approach was one of an endeavor to extract something from God. Sacrifice was offered, even if it was the sacrifice of praise. It was the hope that by this means one might oneself be blessed.

This seemed to work after a fashion in the experience of people for a while, but gradually the idea began to become prevalent that God was somehow falling down on the job. He wasn't delivering the goods to satisfy human beings. Now, of course, there was a certain amount of truth to this, because the purpose of God is not to satisfy human beings. Such an approach is rather childish. Children often think that the only reason for parents is to satisfy the children, and some parents go along with this. But God doesn't go along with it; not that He is desirous of withholding anything, but He is not going to violate the laws of

His own being, not going to change His own character to suit childish human beings. His character might be said to be a positive character. There is never a moment when God is not offering throughout the whole cosmos—not only with respect to this little speck of a planet and the minute people upon it—all that is necessary to the fullest possible experience of life. But, of course, for a long time there has been scarcely any recognition of this on the part of human beings, and in any case they want to have things their own way. They want to design the world around them to suit themselves; and God does not go along with this, because man and the planet upon which he dwells are not isolated from all the rest of the cosmos, and consequently there cannot rightly be function which ignores the requirements in the cosmos as a whole.

So, in any case, man began to feel that God was somehow shortchanging him, or possibly He didn't really exist at all. There seemed to be the necessity, then, of handling human desires, the fulfilment of human satisfaction, in some other way. Self-centeredness had been prevalent in the attitude toward God and, of course, continued to be prevalent when the attention began to wander from God into other areas from whence it was supposed the true blessings might be brought to man.

There was a man who lived quite a long time ago now, a man named Daniel, famous for the lions' den. He was one of those from the Israelites who were carried away captive into Babylon, and he served, while he was there, in various places of authority in the kingdom. In fact, he served under various kings, Nebuchadnezzar amongst them. He was recognized as being a man of character, someone who could be trusted, and so he rose to a prominent position in the land, not only from the standpoint of one king but from the standpoint of all those kings whom he served. So obviously he had something. There were others, of course, with him who also shared positions of responsibility in the kingdom. You may recall the names: Shadrach, Meshach and Abed-nego.

In any case, the Book of Daniel in the Old Testament outlines something of the experiences of Daniel and of his clarity of vision, keen perception, and ability to handle himself wisely both in the sight of God and in the sight of the king. Daniel was also called a prophet. He became aware of certain things that were working out from the historical standpoint. He saw the trends and understood what it was that was unfolding in the affairs of men. While much of what he wrote in this book is couched in symbolical language, it gives, nevertheless, rather a clear outline of what should occur in the days to come. I would like to quote a few verses toward the end of the Book of Daniel, when he was speaking of what might well be called the latter days. A number of kings are described in the presentation which he gave, and a king in the Bible symbolizes the mind of man which tries to rule on earth—rarely in subjection to God; nevertheless the authority of rulership is claimed by man through his mind. These kings are indications of the various levels of consciousness at which human beings function and have functioned all down through the ages. So we come to the latter days. This could very easily refer to the time in which we ourselves live, as I think will be rather clearly portrayed through what he has to say about this particular king.

"And the king shall do according to his will"—that's quite usual, isn't it?—"and he shall exalt himself, and magnify himself above every god, and shall speak marvellous things against the God of gods, and shall prosper till the indignation be accomplished: for that that is determined shall be done.

"Neither shall he regard the God of his fathers, nor

the desire of women, nor regard any god: for he shall magnify himself above all."

Here we have reference to the mind of man where the human intellect becomes supreme, which is the very general experience in the world as we know it, and in our own lives. Because of developments in various fields the mind has increasingly considered itself to be supreme, and everybody has accepted identification pretty well with this god. "Neither shall he regard the God of his fathers, nor the desire of women." This particular statement relates to that delicate perception of true values, of spiritual things, which is present and available to the experience of human beings. But this is set aside, covered up, not attended to, because primary consideration is given to what the intellect says; that overrules everything else and the quality of experience known to human beings everywhere is based in this. Not too many people are satisfied with that quality.

"But in his estate shall he honour the God of forces. . . ."

Power is an emphasized word today. We have black power, red power, white power, student power, political power, economic power, nuclear power. All kinds of power are honored by this god, by the intellect. By the activation of these various areas of power, the mind of man imagines that it is going to rule effectively and successfully. All that really happens is that we have an increase of contention, an increase of conflict, because one aspect of power vies with another aspect of power and everybody wants to be the supreme power. So the human mind in people, even perhaps in you at times, honors the god of forces. Something is going to be imposed by the intellect of man.

". . . and a god whom his fathers knew not shall he honour with gold, and silver, and with precious stones, and pleasant things."

What is this god which is so honored? The god of

scientific and technological achievement. In this fashion man is going to get what he wants. The God of old, the One who was called Almighty God at one time, was not delivering the goods to man as man thought He should, so man proceeds to collect the goods himself on the basis of setting himself up as the supreme god—the intellect of man. Seeing that human beings are identified with their intellects, this is man at the supreme point. On this basis, by reason of his godliness, he is going to be able to get what he wants. Science plus technology is going to be the source of supply, the cow that he is going to milk to obtain the cream of life experience.

"Thus shall he do in the most strong holds with a strange god, whom he shall acknowledge and increase with glory: and he shall cause them to rule over many, and shall divide the land for gain."

Of course, this is all part of the commercial pattern too, isn't it? The land is divided for gain, the whole world, because of the rulership of this king.

Earlier in the story of Daniel's experience with King Nebuchadnezzar, the king had built an image, you may recall. He had had a dream before, but this was an image that he actually built. It was an improvement upon the one he saw in his dream. The one he saw in his dream had a golden head and a silver torso, and brass was included and iron and clay, so he was going to improve on it. He made his image, the one he actually built, all of gold; it was completely made of gold. This is the value, isn't it? Of course, we are more enlightened now; we don't use the gold standard as we used to; we use the paper standard. But it's the same thing. Value is placed where it doesn't belong, and this tremendous image has been built on earth, the world over, purely of gold.

Nebuchadnezzar gathered all the men of authority out of his kingdom for the dedication of this image, and he instructed them that everyone was to bow down and worship this image whenever the music played. In the story various instruments were indicated, which is an interesting thing because evidently they didn't have a word for orchestra, or brass band, whatever it was. But whenever the music played, everybody was to bow down and worship this image on the pain of death—on the pain anyway of extreme discomfort. There was a furnace prepared and anyone who didn't bow down was to be cast into that furnace. This is very descriptive of present-day experience, because when the human intellect plays the tune we are all supposed, if not to bow down to it, to dance to it anyway, to accept the supremacy of this great image of gold. Now some people accept that supremacy because they think they are going to get something out of it. Some people contend with that supremacy because they don't like it, they think it's wrong; but even those who contend with it find that their continued existence on earth is very much dependent upon it. So, increasingly, praise has been given to the god of the intellect, to man himself. "Oh, what a great civilization we live in! Oh, what tremendous things the intellect has done! See the scientific and technological advancement there is. Honor this god. From this god all the blessings of heaven are coming!" And virtually everybody bows down and worships him, worships the image which the human intellect has set up.

Worshiping this, honoring this, people become ashamed of the true God. Shame is never a creative motivation. We may awaken to the fact that we have been suffering from shame, and it is well that we should, but having so awakened we would not wish to perpetuate the situation, because we cannot do anything that is going to be of the smallest value if we are subject to shame, if we are controlled by our sense of shame either with respect to ourselves or somebody else. Some children are ashamed of their parents apparently. Some parents are ashamed of their children. When this is the case, parents and/or children are governed by shame. What they do is based on this shame. The way they behave is based on this shame instead of being right behavior simply because it is right behavior.

Right behavior includes praise to God, praise to what is honorable and true and right. When a person is governed by that, he is beginning to worship the true God and the intellect begins to be dethroned. In the outworking with Nebuchadnezzar he was dethroned at one point. He landed up out in the field eating grass like a cow. He became an animal, which is just about what man has become—man as a whole—simply because false gods are honored and the intellect of man is proclaimed to be the supreme one. Regardless of this futile fancy, the true God remains the true God even though unknown to man. The true God is a reality, but does not exist merely for the benefit of man. If the assumption is made that God should be merely for the benefit of man, God ceases to exist to those who have that attitude, because He is nonexistent in that state; God isn't there.

God is there to provide the creative fulfilment universally, and man has the priceless privilege of participating in that creative fulfilment in this little part of the total universe, but only as he worships, magnifies, gives praise to the true God, only as he opens his eyes to see what is honorable in his immediate environment, what gives indication of the reality of manhood or womanhood. As he opens his eyes to this he will begin to see it and, seeing it, it is not at all difficult to praise God, so that not only music or art or architecture is offered in praise of God—certainly not with the expectation that any such things will produce benefit for oneself—but all that we are may be given to the true God without any expectation of reward whatsoever. This is so foreign to the human approach that it seems quite incredible. It seems to be the height of ridiculousness. "How could anyone do this? We all want what we want, after all!" This is smiled upon by society as long as it doesn't go too far. We can go after what we want. We can raise our standard of living, I was going to say—but perhaps I should say, of dying —by putting the human ego at the supreme point. Look at the architecture today. To whose honor is it built? To the honor of the human ego certainly. "Look at the skyline! Oh, my, isn't that magnificent what man can do for his own benefit!" I rather suspect that some of the church edifices that are built nowadays are based in the same approach. "Our church is better than your church. Our architecture proclaims the brilliance of our architects as opposed to yours." Everything is built to the glory of man. This is the king who is described here so accurately.

"And the king shall do according to his will; and he shall exalt himself, and magnify himself above every god." The human ego, fat and magnificent, marvelous! There has been nothing like it on earth before! I am not sure that is true. I don't think there is anything new under the sun insofar as the human ego is concerned. I think it has all been done before. Perhaps not quite the same way, but it has all been done before, and where is it now? A lot of it is right at the bottom of the ocean. What good is it down there? What good is it up here?

"And he shall exalt himself, and magnify himself"— here is self-centeredness supreme, isn't it?—"above every god, and shall speak marvellous things against the God of gods." He is ashamed of the God of gods. ("Nothing could really be achieved on the basis of yielding in love to the God of gods. No, oh no, that's no good; we can't get what we want out of Him. We are just going to get it for ourselves, disregard the God of gods, be ashamed of the God of gods.") "And shall prosper till the indignation be accomplished." Oh, he just has a little rope; he can go just so far; he is not so almighty as he thought. This is permitted to occur as a part of the larger unfoldment of the creative purposes of the God of gods. Man thinks he is doing it all: oh, how great he is! "For that that is determined shall be done."

So here we have a picture which very few human beings would acknowledge as being true, but it is exactly accurate. It is exactly what has happened. Human beings are puffed up with their own importance as human egos on the basis of the marvels that they have accomplished. The honor is given in this direction, to the false gods. Finally, maybe there will be those on earth who are no longer ashamed of the true God. There are people who believe in God, perhaps, but they keep quiet about it. It needs to come out into the open, you know. It seems foolishness in the sight of man, and the human ego feels ashamed of being foolish in the sight of others. Seeming to be foolish is the correct way of putting it; actually being wise. Obviously, if anyone is governed by what somebody else is going to think about him he is not worshiping the true God, because that somebody else is not the true God. Let us consider what is honorable and true and right, what is the evidence of true character, wherever it may appear, and honor that. Even if it appears right next to you, honor that! People like to honor things way over there somewhere, generally speaking because only when it is way over there does it look honorable. If it gets too close, my, it's not quite so honorable as it looked when it was way out there. People nowadays are very much concerned about building their images, political images and this sort of thing, so that everybody can look and honor that. But it isn't the person at all. Let us find what we may rightly honor right next to us and honor that. Certainly don't be ashamed of it! That is dishonesty, self-deception, and leads to disaster.

Do you know what it says of this king finally?

"And he shall plant the tabernacles of his palace between the seas in the glorious holy mountain; yet he shall come to his end, and none shall help him."

No monument for him! That's what happens to the human intellect; it comes to its end and none shall help it. It's been doing it for years, but people don't pay much attention; whereas the God of gods remains. The honorable state remains. The reality of love remains. The truth remains. Life remains. The evidence of the God of gods throughout the whole universe remains. But the human ego vanishes like a puff of smoke. It doesn't amount to anything. Oh, how difficult it is for human beings to reach a point where they are willing to acknowledge this, that they may come again to themselves, to the beauty of being which is above the human intellect, come again to the realization of the mature state of divine manhood or womanhood, true self-consciousness which does not require the support of the human ego to exist. The fact of the matter is that the human ego itself only exists because the true self is present. When the human ego has thoroughly separated itself from the true self it has ceased to exist.

Let us rejoice and praise the Lord! He is good! He is just wonderful! His character is beyond the imaginings of the human intellect. The fulfilment in the experience of true being is undreamed of insofar as the mind of man in its ego state is concerned. But it's here waiting to be experienced when we give honor to what is honorable and only to that. We don't give honor simply to avoid being cast into the fire and becoming a bit uncomfortable. Anyone who is true to himself is cast into the fire, that is true, but if a person is true to himself, as Shadrach, Meshach and Abed-nego found out, the fire doesn't burn them. It's all just wonderful. All it does is to clarify the situation and the individual is released to be himself. His bonds are burned, that's all. And, finally, let us recall what Shadrach, Meshach and Abed-nego said to King Nebuchadnezzar, said to the human ego which tries to get people to honor it, no matter in whom it may appear:

"Shadrach, Meshach, and Abed-nego answered and said to the king, O Nebuchadnezzar, we are not careful to answer thee in this matter." We are not going to shilly-shally around!

"If it be so, our God whom we serve is able to deliver us from the burning fiery furnace, and he will deliver us out of thine hand, O king." That is a very definite statement: He will do that. Whether He delivers from the state of discomfort or not is beside the point; He will deliver the person from subjection to the king.

"But if not, be it known unto thee, O king, that we will not serve thy gods, nor worship the golden image which thou hast set up."

How about being just as definite as that? That's the only way we ever come clear. That's the only way we ever grow up, the only way we ever find the maturity of true self-consciousness. As long as we are shilly-shallying around, being pulled here and pulled there by what somebody thinks or somebody else doesn't think, blinding ourselves to the truth, to what is honorable and right and loving that—there is nothing more beautiful than that anyway—as long as that is the case we remain in slavery. We never know what it is to be free. Let us choose this day whom we are to serve: the honorable God or the puffed-up ego. Where's the choice? There is only one thing, and how beautiful that one thing is! How delighted we are when we have made that choice to praise God in every conceivable way, in all our words, in all our ways. While maybe we don't go around panning the human ego, we are very conscious of the real nature of that ego and we are not in the least interested in it. When it gives forth with its music, the last thing we do is fall down and worship, the last thing we do is to allow what we do to be governed by that dishonorable thing. So we may be restored to honesty, to rightness, to beauty, to glory, giving praise to God in the highest. Glory to God in the highest now and always!

No!

Besides being a service again this morning in which we have the opportunity of serving, we also have the opportunity of learning. Our learning, as our serving, will be to the extent that we share the creative process by which form is given to spirit, specifically to the spirit of truth, the spirit of God. As we share this creative process, we share in the learning. That learning is not based in an arbitrary instruction emanating from the one who speaks to you, but it is nevertheless instruction offered by the spirit of God and known by us as we permit that spirit to be clothed in form. What I say is then also what you say; there is agreement. This is the only basis, of course, for true agreement.

If we recognize this, then obviously the real values are in spirit. We remain eternally ignorant if we ignore this fact. Unfortunately, human beings are inclined to ignore the fact while at the same time assuming that they know it all. We never come to know it all, in any case, but the only way that we can know what needs to be known is by putting our values in spirit where the source of true knowing is, so that we may participate in the creative process by which invisible, unknown spirit may take form through us. If we see this as being so, all true learning is then recognized as being wrapped up with spirit. The understanding comes through spirit, not through analysis of form, and certainly not through desires with respect to form.

Man, male and female, was created in the image and likeness of God. While maybe there are those who might dispute this point because they say there isn't a God, nevertheless if it is true that man was made in the image and likeness of God, then man is a spiritual being and not merely a material being. He does not know himself and consequently he does not, in fact, really know anything, until he discovers that he is a spiritual being. The process of this discovery is the process of maturing. Man is mature when he knows for himself what he is. As long as people are ignorant on this score, per se they are immature. The fact of the matter is that the world is populated by several billions of immature people.

There is the inclination for people to pretend that they know something, that they are mature, in other words, at almost every stage of experience which properly should lead to the reality of maturity, the experience of being spiritual. There is an automatic process, physically speaking, by which the body matures. It doesn't mature because the person decides that this would be desirable; it doesn't stop maturing because the individual decides that it would be nice to remain at some particular level; it occurs automatically. This process works out automatically in relationship to all living forms, but there is something to man that properly sets him apart from the animal kingdom, the kingdom of vegetation and the mineral kingdom. This which so sets him apart is the capacity to experience his spiritual reality consciously. The fact of the matter is that all living forms, all forms in fact, reveal the truth of spirit. If we are considering animals, they function on the basis of being spiritual without knowing it. The same is true of the kingdom of vegetation and also, in fact, the mineral kingdom, because nothing would exist if it were not for spirit. However, man, having the capacity to know that he is spiritual, has failed to mature to that point, consequently tending to accept his material experience as being what he is. He knows himself as a material being, consequently he is in a worse plight than all the rest of creation which, while revealing the fact that it is spiritual, doesn't know it and therefore cannot deny it. But man is capable of denying the truth, which he has done very consistently, and consequently refused to mature.

The true creative process should proceed in the natural cycles of physical maturing so that man matures spiritually at the same time. This starts off all right, to a certain extent. A baby has no consciousness of anything much. There is a spiritual being there, sometimes recognized by others; they might say, "a gift from heaven," something very sweet and beautiful, uninhibited, clear, so that the light shines through, so to speak, this little physical form, and that stirs the hearts of those who observe. But the baby doesn't know it. However, after a while there begins to be the development of what we call self-consciousness; it comes gradually.

That self-consciousness is, to start with, of a young child presumably. Most of us have matured, physically speaking at least, beyond that point. We can look back and recall that we were a baby; we must have been. Perhaps our memory is not too vivid on that point but usually there is some remembrance of certain events, in any case, when we were quite young. We had a certain experience of ourselves back there but we certainly didn't stay at that experience, did we? We proceeded from that point. We had the self-consciousness of a child, which was all right at that point—rather self-centered, of course, which also was all right at that point. Gradually, as physical growth continued there was also the growth in the experience of self-consciousness. We became conscious of being a boy or girl, as the case might be, and at that point this was everything to us; we had no experience beyond that point. Yet subsequently we have had experience beyond that point. We passed through the teen-age time. I suppose during that period we thought we knew quite a bit. We had the experience of being that, and yet those of us who have moved beyond that point know that wasn't the end and that we didn't really know it all during that period.

Possibly, in the processes of maturing, if we really had been moving toward spiritual maturity, we became increasingly aware of how little we knew. Perhaps this is one of the evidences of a continued experience in the maturing process. We may have been rather brash know-it-alls at some points along the way, but later we discovered that that was rather foolish, because the more we really know the more we realize how little we know. The process of maturing spiritually does actually bring us increasingly to the realization of how little we know. That's what should happen! Unfortunately, all too many try to carry forward that brash know-it-all viewpoint out of the teen-age into the adult experience, so that they live in this conceited pretense. If a person is really honest with himself he knows that he doesn't know, but he tries to fool himself and fool others as to how much he knows.

We have a stratified experience here, don't we, which relates to this concern that so many have had with respect to what they call lack of communication, because seemingly people can only communicate with their peers, so to speak, those who are at the same level as themselves. This isn't real communication at all, actually, because they are communicating about things they don't know anything about, never having matured spiritually so as to reach a point of genuinely not knowing, so that the true knowing might begin to emerge, the true knowing which springs from spirit, the spirit of God. The experience of true knowing is the experience of letting spirit take form through us; therefore until we mature spiritually we really know nothing, and to admit that we know nothing is the first evidence of wisdom, because we may then place ourselves in position where we can begin to know something by reason of the fact that spirit is being clothed in form through us.

This movement to a true experience of spiritual self-consciousness, which is true self-consciousness, works out through certain cycles naturally. There needs to be an awareness of the fact that it is properly working out in this fashion and that no experience, until we reach the point of spiritual self-consciousness, is mature. We are immature all along the line. If we try to pretend that we are mature we are self-deceived, and if we try to act on the basis of our supposed maturity we get into trouble. In these cycles of true growing up our experience of ourselves changes, so we are wise enough never to assume that our experience of ourselves at any particular point is the final word. It certainly isn't unless we make it so, and if we make it so for ourselves at any point, we cease to mature in the true sense of the word; we get stuck at some level of immaturity.

The basis for true communication is a spiritual one. It isn't communication between peers in the material sense. I suppose we could say it's communication between peers in the spiritual sense, the word "peers" indicating equals or those who are at the same level as we are. There is only one true level of maturity and that is spiritual maturity, where the individual realizes his spiritual reality, that he is not just a material form with a few appendages of mental or emotional ability. There is a very definite consciousness of spiritual self to be known when a person really moves into the experience of maturity. Of course it's not just a stepping over the one line and saying, "Now I am mature," because there is a continuing unfoldment in this regard. Spiritual being is not a finished product in the sense that when you have experienced yourself as a spiritual being there is nothing more; that would be deadly. Spirit unfolds in expression of itself eternally; there is no end to it. So there is no end to the experience of maturity. There is no end to the self-consciousness of being spiritual.

However, to reach that point we necessarily pass through the growing-up stages. In relationship to those growing-up stages there is one particular aspect which is basically a key, when we begin to see it, which allows us continually to open the doors from stage to stage in the maturing process so that we do not blindly insist upon maintaining a limited experience of self. This key was illustrated for us in the long ago through what have been called the Ten Commandments. Most people have noted that the Ten Commandments relate to negatives. You know, the little two-letter word No is fundamentally the key. Obviously, where there is a No there is also a Yes, a nice little three-letter word. Yes, "thou shalt love the Lord thy God." The Noes relate to many things. There is just one Yes fundamentally, but the Noes relate to many things.

Now, parents are very much aware of the fact that when their babies start to grow they begin to be able to crawl and walk around and they get into everything. If a parent is not careful he finds himself constantly saying "No!" So there is a need to provide a setting as far as possible where it is not necessary to say "No"; merely from the standpoint of the fact that if this is not done there will be an almost continuous No. There will be sufficient No if the setting is of such a nature that the necessity for saying No is reduced to the minimum; there will be plenty still. If No is said too much it tends to establish a "thing" in the consciousness of the child with respect to the little word No. But obviously, if it is necessary to say No to a baby growing up, that is part of the maturing process, and the little word No is an essential word in the maturing process. Nobody can ever mature without the use of that little word or without the fact of what the little word conveys.

If it is seen to be desirable—one might say here is the goal, the beautiful, wonderful goal of being on earth—to reach the point of spiritual maturity, then there will be an increasing experience of an attitude of delight with respect to this little word No, because it leads to the point of maturity. It doesn't lead to the point of maturity if there is only No. There must be Yes too, but the Yes fundamentally relates to the first great commandment; in other words, "Yes, I am moving toward the point of spiritual maturity; yes, it is my greatest and deepest desire to grow up!" So we need to see this little word No in its true light and why it was that the Ten Commandments when first given were mostly No: Don't do this, don't do that! There was a Yes, obviously, there: "Thou shalt have no other gods before me." Even that one was put on the basis of a No. "Yes, thou shalt have Me as the only God," in other words, and because of that the controls in life will not be material controls, and the Noes relate to this.

A young person growing up, of course, will find many things that are seemingly desirable: "I want to do this!" There is the necessity, properly speaking, if that person is ever to grow up, for a parent or somebody else to say No, presumably on the right occasions, not just a blanket No to everything. But the reason for this No is not so much related to what the person wants to do, although that comes into the picture, of course, and will determine where the Noes can be rightly applied, but to enable that person to learn to take No, to accept No; because if a person, during the process of physical maturing, does not concurrently mature spiritually it's going to be tougher later on, as some of you could testify. One needs to learn how to accept No with a good grace, we might say, so that there is not instant rebellion with respect to it, because that rebellion, although it isn't seen so, is a rebellion against the process of growing up, of maturing. A person has to learn to accept the word No from somebody else in order to learn to accept it from himself.

Those who have had longer experience of living in this world have discovered that there are many, many Noes, not just from the standpoint of somebody saying No to you but from the standpoint of the circumstances themselves. They say No loud and clear very often, and that's that! If you do not know how to accept that No, then there's an awful lot of stewing going on inside, disturbance and trouble, conflict. The individual is all hung up in that, making no progress toward maturity. All too many people grow up into adulthood physically speaking while remaining entirely childish on this score: they do not know how to handle the little word No.

We can all look back to rather vivid experiences in earlier years, perhaps some quite recently, where we were under the necessity of accepting the word No. I can look back to that quite easily, until, I recall, one time it occurred to me that it probably was harder for my parents to say No than it was for me to accept the No. But, you know, these two aspects of the No go together: A person who has never learned to accept No for himself can't say No to anybody else. There is this cockeyed notion, so popular in recent years, that if you ever say No it's going to frustrate somebody and he is going to grow up twisted. Well, we have a generation rather recently growing up where No has not been said much and we find something that isn't entirely untwisted. It has nothing to do with the concepts that people have along these lines; it is just simply the fact of the matter, that unless a person can keep the Ten Commandments, so to speak, on the basis of No and feel good about it, he will never, never reach the point of spiritual maturity; he will never grow up.

Sometimes, of course, I suppose quite frequently in this upside-down world in which we live, the Noes that people utter are seemingly unfair or unjust, but that again is not the point. A lot of people try to make a big thing out of that but that is not the point. The point is as to whether the person to whom the No is given is capable of accepting that No in the right attitude. That's the point, because if the person has learned that—and it doesn't really matter if the No is just or unjust; he can learn it in either case—he has allowed the key which opens the door to maturity to begin to be used. It is not a matter of accepting the No on the surface and rebelling and stewing inside about it underneath. That person is not growing up; that person is insisting upon maintaining the identity of an immature person. Of course if he does that too long it tends to become an ingrained habit, and we see all sorts of people with many, many years under their belts functioning on this basis. Oh, they get so mad because somebody said No, or the circumstance said No. They can't take it; they don't know how to handle it. They never grew up to that point. So why not take advantage of the Noes that are offered, seeing them as opportunities of moving in the cycle of maturing? Instead of seeing the No as a cause for stewing about it we see the No as a cause for delight, because here is the opportunity to handle it rightly. And the person who does it grows up, provided that he has the true Yes.

Now, of course, the fact of the matter is that he won't be able to handle the No rightly unless he has the right Yes. The right Yes, as we have seen, relates to this process of becoming a true man or a true woman; for men and women, made in the image and likeness of God, are spiritual beings. God is spirit; man is spirit, made in the image and likeness of God. Most people think of man being made in the image and likeness of God from the standpoint of the material factors. The material factors are included because they are a reflection of whatever it is that is established in spirit; they do not exist of themselves. But the true sense of self is a spiritual one, and that spiritual sense of self comes as a person moves in the cycles of maturing, not assuming that mere physical maturing produces automatically the maturity of a man or a woman. It certainly doesn't. It makes that experience of maturity possible, and it does that automatically, which is a wonderful thing. In other words, the possibility of true maturity is provided for everybody by reason of the fact of physical maturity, but to mature spiritually requires a deliberate choice.

The animals, the plants, mature spiritually at their own levels of experience automatically; they have no choice in the matter. They reveal themselves for what they are, spiritually speaking. Man has to make a deliberate choice because from his standpoint spiritual maturity is a conscious experience. He is not an automaton. It is a conscious experience which must be deliberately and willingly accepted, and he will find that in that acceptance, in that Yes, he has to learn how to handle the Noes both from the standpoint of the Noes that come to him and from the standpoint of the Noes that move through him into the world. We all have the responsibility of saying No when that is the right thing to say, and we will never handle that responsibility wisely or well until we have learned how to accept No with respect to ourselves, because we have no true No to give unless we have accepted it. This is the fact with respect to all that finds expression through us of the spirit of God. Unless we accept it in relationship to ourselves in the control of our own lives we have no provision of spiritual reality to extend to anybody else.

So I emphasize this key which, indeed, was emphasized for us long ago when the Ten Commandments were given: No! Here was a people coming out of slavery, under the necessity of growing up to take responsibility for themselves, and the first requirement was No. Oh, how human beings rebel against No. They want to do what they want to do. "Nobody's going to tell me no!" Poor you! If you fight against that all your life you remain childish, for one thing, and you have a miserable existence, for another; for there are many what we might call automatic Noes, and there is a final No, you know: thus far and no further. If we have learned to accept the No as we move through the cycles of maturing, we can accept that final No with good grace if it should come.

Our treasure is a spiritual treasure. Our treasure is in heaven, rightly. Our values are properly there because we ourselves are properly there. If we put our values anywhere else we are downgrading ourselves. Our only true value is as a spiritual being. A spiritual being is an eternal being. A material being is a very temporal being. So here is the nature of the maturing process, and one of the primary elements by which we are enabled to know it.

The Passing of Restrictions

What deep delight and tremendous excitement there is in the experience of being with one accord in one place! As long as this remained only an idea of the mind it seemed to be rather a flat business, but when it comes alive because we experience something of the truth of it, how very wonderful that is. We have certainly touched something of this on occasion. We just enjoy one another's company without being particularly aware of each other but simply of the shared experience, what has been called the outpouring of the spirit. That outpouring is not a figment of fancy. It does not come on stereotyped lines according to the concepts of men but is known as a living reality, something which words cannot really describe.

The creative power of God which moves so constantly throughout the whole universe is known to us in our own personal experience. It is no longer a theoretical concept about something out there, but we touch the truth of it in ourselves and we know that it is moving in us, that anything that finds expression in our living is consequent upon that movement. We also recognize that most of what we have known has been on the basis of a mistranslation of the power inherently within which is the design and the control for our experience, just as surely as for the experience of the whole universe. Obviously, if there has been this mistranslation—and the very circumstances around us reveal that it is so—then there have been what are called inhibitions.

There are those who, recognizing the fact of inhibition in human experience, imagine that the true expression of life would appear if those inhibitions were somehow dissolved. There are those, of course, who try to function on this basis. They are going to do what they imagine to be their thing, regardless of anyone or anything. The idea is that we must be ourselves. Of course, there is a basic truth to this, but do you suppose that if we were in position to let all inhibitions be dissolved the result would be the kingdom of heaven on earth? The point is that the pollution of the subconscious waters is not merely what is floating around on the surface. The water is polluted to depth, and if we just remove the surface rubbish, that may permit something to come up from the depths all right, but it will still be pollution; it will still be the distorted mistranslation of the creative compulsion, the tide of movement which is of God. So it is well that we should have a few inhibitions. The subterranean eruptions which might appear if the inhibitions were not there would likely be far more destructive than the inhibitions are; so the answer certainly is not in what people have imagined to be free expression. Free expression through human beings as they now are is bound to be a mess. There is a purifying and cleansing process required so that the waters may be clear, may become a sea of glass clear as crystal. That isn't the case at once in anyone.

So we are not particularly anxious to dissolve all the surface inhibitions, because what would come out from the subsurface levels would be no better. Our concern is rightly to seek first the kingdom of God and His righteousness, not to leap into realms of unknown imagination where we think that we could give expres-

sion to something pure and wonderful suddenly. We
have those who have functioned as though this could
be done, and it doesn't work, even in church. There
are some who have been called "the holy rollers," for
instance, because of the antics they go through on the
basis of the temporary relinquishment of inhibitions in
church. Of course, the fact of being in church still
maintains some of the inhibitions, but peculiar things
happen; certainly not any evidence of the design and
the control of the creative power of God, which
doesn't operate in a foolish manner nor cause human
beings to do foolish things.

The point really is that there is no such thing as the
experience of freedom without the reality of design
and control. The human concept often is, with respect
to freedom, that it is a matter of throwing off all control. Sometimes young people imagine that that is
freedom—when they can throw off all parental control, for instance. Then they will be free as the air. We
have a lot of young people who are trying this out
these days but it isn't freedom. It may be a form of license, which is always destructive in the end.

When we are responsible for caring for a young
child we would not imagine it to be sensible to let that
young child have his way in everything. This is no
condemnation of the child; it is merely the course of
wisdom on the part of the parent. A baby who is just
learning to crawl, or even walk, will wish to get into
everything, try out everything; consequently there is
the necessity for providing a certain protective control. We wouldn't think it sensible to permit that child
to do whatever he wanted. He would either be crip-
pled or dead very shortly. So control is rightly exerted
in such case. Gradually, as the child grows, he will develop the capacity to stand, for instance, and walk. A
child who has not developed that capacity yet has to

be watched quite carefully, but as the child can be trusted to stand he can be trusted to do more things; to have a greater freedom, in other words, because the control essential to standing and walking has been accepted. The acceptance of the control necessary to stand and to walk permits freedom. If it were imagined that freedom is simply the experience of doing whatever one wants, then one would never need to learn to stand and walk. You could spend your whole life on your hands and knees, completely free! That would hardly be freedom, would it? We find it much freer in our experience to be able to stand and walk.

In every step of the increased experience of freedom there is the acceptance of an increased experience of design and control. In other words, the experience of true freedom is consequent upon the acceptance of design and control. There is no freedom without it. Now in the upbringing of a child this principle is recognized, if not put into exact words, because gradually as the child becomes more trustworthy and learns to be obedient—not to play with matches for instance—then the child can be given freedom in the area where the matches are. If there is not the development of that trustworthiness, then the child must be restricted to that extent. That restriction prevents the experience of freedom, not because it is a restriction but because the child has not learned to accept the design and the control which would make it possible to remove that restriction.

At any age in the process of growth toward maturity there is the necessity for maintaining a certain pattern of control in the external sense until the person has become trustworthy at the particular level of growth. This is not limited to what we call childhood or even youth. It is not finished at the age of twenty-one. It is not finished at the age of ninety-one. There is always more where the person has not yet experienced the application of design and control in his own life. Consider yourselves, regardless of your age physically speaking. Do you imagine that you have accepted as yet the fulness of the design and the control of the spirit of God? To the extent that this has not been your experience, to that extent you must rightly be restricted. You can't be trusted with the freedom which would be known if you had accepted the essential design and control. So this is something that we can see quite easily with respect to a young baby. For the protection of that child there must be certain restrictions in order that the child might grow to the next level, not be eliminated in the first level. Well, we can be eliminated in any level, and will be to the extent that we do not accept the essential restrictions until we have learned to be trustworthy at that level. Then the restrictions can be taken off but only because we ourselves have accepted for ourselves the design and the control that are operative at that particular level. Because we have accepted that, we are completely free to function on that basis. That is freedom but it only comes because of the design and the control that are accepted by the person. "And ye shall know the truth, and the truth shall make you free." The two elements of truth are design and control.

If there is design there are always certain limits. Can you image a design that had no limits? We have the design of a car, for instance, and it has its limits. We don't feel cheated because the car has limits. I don't think we would be very appreciative of a car that didn't have limits. We would never know what was going to happen. But we have a definite awareness of usefulness and value in a car because it has certain limits. In our own designs there are limits. In the design of our physical bodies there are limits; we don't ooze all over the place. Our bodies stay put together in the design, and that's quite all right. We can be effective because of that.

There are limits in the sense of design as it applies to external objects and also limits with respect to design as it applies to operational function. It is important that there should be these limits; otherwise there couldn't be control. There is a certain operating design to us individually speaking and an operating design insofar as the whole body of mankind is concerned. As individuals and as a whole we cannot experience freedom without the acceptance of whatever that design is. If we try to do away with the design we engender chaos.

Of course, most people, insofar as the collective body is concerned, are unaware of what the design might be. They have set it up on the basis of a human organization. We have nations, for instance, in the total design. The nations themselves have internal design. These are the collective inhibitions, aren't they? And there are those who think that it would be a good idea to do away with those inhibitions, overthrow the design by one means or another, mostly by force. Of course, when you overthrow a design there is chaos until another design appears somehow. This is the idea, of course, very often with people: the design that we now have is wrong but they think they have a better idea. "Do away with the present design and we will put a new one in!" But this is all part of the rejection of the true design, the substitution of a false design for the true one, because the true design can only be experienced as people are willing to mature.

There are many young people who exhibit an unwillingness to mature. They are not alone in this. Some of the older people do this too; most of them in fact. But the concept is that the rejection of design is part of the process of maturing. That is absolute nonsense! The only way anyone can experience maturity is by the acceptance of the true design and the true control. The true design and the true control are not humanly invented. The design is a reality already, as is the control. It may be accepted or rejected. If it is rejected we must remain childish, untrustworthy, incapable of functioning correctly as mature men and women. A child who remains in a baby state, refusing to grow up, would cause a great deal of damage both to himself and to others, and this is basically what human beings have done. They have remained childish, rejecting the true design and control, endeavoring to substitute their own, and they wreck themselves and everybody else.

"Seek ye first the kingdom of God, and his righteousness." Coming into the awareness of the reality of the true design and the true control in actual experience is the process of maturing. It can't be done, nobody can mature, as long as they are trying to set up their own designs and their own controls—or lack of them, as the case may be. How sensible, then, to seek first the kingdom of God, the government that is already present, in its design and control aspects, and the right state of experience which is consequent upon the acceptance of the kingdom. "Thy kingdom come," many people have prayed hopefully, but insisted upon rejecting it, ignorantly perhaps but just as certainly.

Now, we begin to see and to understand these things so that we may accept the design and the control which are already present. In order to reach that point there must be a willingness to be restricted until we have proven trustworthiness. A child is restricted from the use of matches until he has proven that he can be trusted with them. Then he is free to use them because on that basis he will not use them indiscriminately to burn the house down. He will use them for, presumably, constructive purposes if he uses them at all. Of course, a child who is restricted from using matches always wants to use matches. That's the way human beings behave. Certain restrictions are placed upon them by the very circumstances in which they find themselves and they tend to rebel against the restrictions instead of learning what it means to become trustworthy so that the restrictions are not necessary. Once the restrictions are removed because the individual becomes trustworthy he is not hankering all the time to use the matches. There is no particular attraction to it any more. But the individual who uses restrictions as a reason for rebellion can never grow up. When he sees restrictions as a means by which he may learn trustworthiness he has no reason to rebel against the restrictions because, learning trustworthiness, the restrictions are dissolved.

There are humanly imposed restrictions of various sorts about which people feel badly and to which they object, and restrictions of this sort very often are thought of as being causes of frustration. But, you know, we can accept them gracefully. This relates to the matter of the No, doesn't it, that we were considering recently. We can accept No gracefully, or if we don't accept the No gracefully, or at all, and get into trouble because of that, then we can accept the trouble gracefully. For instance, some find the speed limit restricting when they are driving down the highway and they may go beyond it to some extent. But if the cop with the radar is around the corner, then we are brought to task; rightly so, on the basis of that particular restriction. We need to accept the situation gracefully. People do a lot of things that violate the law—restrictions that are self-imposed insofar as the body politic is concerned—and then feel badly done by because they are hurt in some fashion by reason of their own actions. Of course, sometimes people like to be martyrs in this respect to benefit some cause or other, but what futility! We see something going on in

Northern Ireland these days that to anyone who stands back far enough from it looks absolutely ridiculous; which, of course, it is. But it's tragically ridiculous. Those who are involved in it take it all very seriously, rebelling against restrictions of various kinds, and they behave childishly in consequence, because you can't rebel against restriction and mature at the same time.

The thing to do is to learn to be a trustworthy man or woman in the circumstance exactly the way it is. That permits a person to mature. In maturing, an influence will be exerted into that circumstance the way it was so that the circumstance changes one way or another, but not on the basis of trying to change it arbitrarily. We have people all over the world earnestly and sincerely dedicating their lives to battling restrictions, dedicating their lives to staying childish.

Let us recognize a distinction here between knowledgeableness and maturity. People nowadays are supposedly better educated than they used to be, or at least more people are educated. Many of those who have some sort of education imagine that the fact of an education makes for maturity. That is definitely not true of what is called education in the world that we now know. It does not make for maturity. There may conceivably be some mature educated people, but precious few, and they are not mature because they were educated. There are some who are very much concerned because in their young days they never received an education. Very often it is someone who has achieved a measure of success in the world without an education. He is all the time thinking how much more he could have achieved if he had had an education. It is just possible that if he had had an education he wouldn't have achieved anything. Maybe it was the fact that he didn't have an education that was the trigger which made possible the achievement. But usually such a person says, "I won't let my children grow up without an education, so that they don't have the disadvantages that I had." But how did he know that what he had was a disadvantage? It may actually have been an advantage.

There is a vast difference between being educated and being mature. A person may have his head full of all kinds of knowledge and be very proficient in many fields, an expert maybe, but be absolutely childish. Because there has been the tendency to worship the human intellect, these educated children have been the gods. They have never learned how not to play with matches. If we have a world full of children who do not know how to use matches constructively, and they dissolve restrictions on the use of matches, it will not be surprising if the house is set on fire. That's the world in which we live, because it is peopled by these childish creatures who think of themselves as being adult human beings. We have been included in the number. We grow up when we see the necessity for restrictions on children, when we see the necessity for restrictions at every level in the process of maturing.

When a young child wants to do things that would be dangerous to him he doesn't know that they would be dangerous to him; he doesn't know that. And usually a young child will take restrictions all in good part. He is going after something or other and mother comes along, lifts him up and takes him away. She plunks him down some place else and he happily goes after something else, forgets about the other thing. But as the child grows up he is not quite so amenable as a rule and increasingly he wants to do what he wants to do, thinking that he knows what he is doing. But the same principle applies at that level. There are those things which that individual doesn't know, just as there were for the little baby. It is a disastrous state of affairs when human beings dissolve their restrictions, as they have tended to try to do in this world. Then someone who is educated says, "Now I am mature; therefore I do not need any restrictions. I can function freely as my intellect tells me how," and that is just as fatal or disastrous to a twenty-, thirty-, forty-, fifty-, sixty-, seventy-, eighty-, ninety-year-old person as it is to a child a year old, at the particular level where the person is, because there are always those things with respect to which he has not yet matured.

Now, of course, from the standpoint of the true design and the true control provision has been made so that there may be the right restrictions on people in the processes of their maturing. Perhaps you can see that as it relates to the story of Adam and Eve. There were certain restrictions during the processes of maturing. But if a person moving through this experience decides one day that now he knows, now he is able to throw off restrictions and function freely as he thinks of it, the result will be disaster. We, generation after generation, have inherited the disaster of that first error, but instead of seeing the error, we have participated in it ourselves and thought up bigger and better ways of erring, of doing what we damned well want to do without regard to restrictions. That's why we have atomic bombs and nuclear weapons and all this sort of thing, of course. That's why we have the sort of world we live in. Human beings don't hear the Noes. If they are stopped by a No they look for a way of getting around it. They don't learn from it; they just look for a way of getting around it. If you don't learn from it you never mature, and so the world is filled with childish people playing with matches.

If we see this in relationship to ourselves we see the value of restrictions. We don't look upon them as bad. We don't look upon them as frustrating. They only become frustrating when we try to get around them. If we accept them gracefully so that we may function in a trustworthy manner in those restrictions—I suppose you could say in spite of them—then there begins to be the beginning of wisdom. We begin to respect the way things really work more than we respect our own educated ideas about it. We see that only in the experience of maturity is there true freedom. When we are mature we can do anything, but because we can do anything doesn't mean that we do do anything. We simply do the thing that is right, the thing that should be done. That is easy and natural because the design and the control of this creative power of God is our own. That's what we are. It is our nature. It is the fact of our being and that's the way we function. We couldn't function any other way. A child can't function as a mature person. He has to pass through the cycles of maturing to reach the point of maturity. That is true of us and of all people. It is, as we have seen, a spiritual experience. This is the way we come to know the truth, and freedom is known at the same time.

In any true spiritual ministry certain restrictions are present. They are not arbitrarily imposed but a person who refuses to accept them will never mature; that's all there is to it. He will remain childish all his days. There are restrictions which necessarily must be accepted. There is a design and there is a control. This is the way it is. The restrictions are, in a sense, arbitrary, even though they have to be accepted voluntarily, until the individual has learned to be trustworthy in relationship to them. The very moment a person is trustworthy in relationship to any restriction the restriction is no longer there. It automatically vanishes. We have had quite a few people who have been associated with this ministry who have complained about the restrictions. They didn't like the restrictions. There are restrictions inherent in the idea of focalization, for instance. To the extent that there was rebellion in this regard the individual was saying, "I refuse to grow up. I refuse to learn to accept what appears to me at the moment, because I am childish, as a particular restriction." But when the individual is trustworthy in that situation, where did the restriction go? It simply isn't there any more because it is no longer translated in the consciousness of the person as a restriction. He is no longer childish.

The individual who has come to know the truth, who has accepted the design and the control of being, is free. There are no more restrictions. He does not translate anything as a restriction in his own consciousness. That's the only way to dissolve restrictions, you know: when they are no longer seen as restrictions. As long as you think they are restrictions they will be restrictions to you. But when you see what they really are they cease to be restrictions; you change your mind. Oh, what wasted energy there is on earth on the part of billions of people who are hammering at restrictions when the fact of the matter is that there are not any there! If those people happened to grow up they would discover the fact, but they keep themselves in the childish state by bucking the restrictions. A child will be inclined to ask, when a restriction is imposed, "Don't you trust me?" Well, the answer to that is another question: "Are you trustworthy?" Never let yourself be put on the defensive, you know. "Are you trustworthy?" That's the point! And a person proves out his trustworthiness or lack of it in ways that he doesn't usually look at. He is looking at the thing that he wants to do but there are always other things related in the pattern where the individual is actually proving whether he is trustworthy or not.

Let's allow the wonderful power of the creative being of God to be used righteously instead of letting it be frittered away in futile endeavors to change the environment, the restrictions. Think of all the force there is in the world that is being used in this moment to buck restrictions! There is no lack of power to permit salvation when it is allowed to be used for that purpose, but it will never be used for that purpose as long as people stay childish. They stay childish basically because they are constantly bucking their restrictions. People feel frustrated and they explain all the reasons as to why they are frustrated. If this thing was changed, well, they wouldn't be frustrated, and all this. Nonsense! They are frustrated because they have chosen to be frustrated by their very attitude to what they call restrictions. "These things are frustrating me!" How do they do it? No, we frustrate ourselves if we are frustrated, by our own attitudes, by the way we look at things, by the names we call things. Restrictions, terrible things! Beautiful things, to be accepted gracefully that we may prove our maturity in relationship to them when we can be trusted to be right in the restrictions. When we prove that we are right in what we have thought of as the restrictions we can be trusted. Where do the restrictions go then? If they are some sort of arbitrary man-made restrictions which we previously thought we didn't like we are not concerned if they don't vanish immediately. Something is going to happen. Something is going to happen when we become men and women and let it happen. The creative power of God is there and it's not a little thing.

So we may share in this process by which we come again to trustworthiness, to maturity, and allow the expression of the creative power of God, governed and right, in the fulfilment of those purposes for which we ourselves are on earth; not something we are forced to do but something we came to do. As we share this we indeed come alive because here is the power of God moving through us. What a delight that is! How exciting that is! We are no longer blocked on every hand by these appalling restrictions, because they simply vanished away. We don't see them as restrictions any more. So let us thank God for the truth that makes men free.

The Salvation of God

Man's internal state is reflected upon the screen of the world around him. If that reflection seems to be disturbing, then the concern should be with man's internal state.

When speaking of man collectively there is a tendency to overlook the fact that man collectively is composed of man individually. It is therefore one's own internal state that should be of concern. It is obvious enough that in the general sense there has been no understanding of this basic principle, that the world outside is a reflection of the world inside, because all of man's energy has been directed toward whatever adjustments seem to be necessary in the world outside. Precious little attention has been paid to the world inside.

If the world outside is apparently filled with violence and conflict and injustice, this being a reflection cannot be changed in any fundamental sense by applying so-called reason or even force to the external pattern. There is a quote often used from the Bible: "Come now, and let us reason together, saith the Lord." So human beings imagine that by reasoning together they are going to achieve something worthwhile. But the word of the Lord was, "Come now, let *us* reason together." It wasn't, "Come now, why don't *you* reason together?" In other words, here is something that relates to the internal state, not the external state. If there are to be constructive changes in the external state they must first appear in the internal state; therefore we may well question as to what is wrong with the internal state rather than what is wrong with the external state. Most people find it quite easy to point to the things that are wrong with the external state, but they do not see quite so clearly, and there is some reluctance, when it comes to the internal state.

If there is a lack of harmony and order in man's external experience in the world, then it is because there is a lack of harmony and order in his individual internal state. Why is there a lack of harmony and order in his individual internal state? When we begin to find the right question we will discover the right answer. As we have before noted, most of the questions that human beings ask are false questions. They are foolish questions. They don't really lead to any true understanding. If you ask a silly question you will receive a silly answer, and this is just about what has been happening in the world of man. All kinds of silly questions are asked and all kinds of silly answers are given. But coming again to basics, we find ourselves to be properly concerned with the internal state of the individual. Which individual? Well, there is only one insofar as each of us is concerned. What is our own internal state? If we are ready to acknowledge that it isn't as healthy as it might be, then we can ask, "Why isn't it as healthy as it might be?" Finally we begin to approach a true answer, simply because we are approaching a true question.

If there is something awry with respect to our internal state, obviously it is because there is a lack of balance somehow. Whatever is inside us in our present experience doesn't adequately fit together in balance. There is conflict internally speaking. Sometimes the battle rages. There is a sense of something wrong, of something not there that should be there. Whatever it is that would bring harmony and balance, a sense of stability and strength internally speaking, is to such a large degree absent. We are aware of a hole, an absence. Something which should be there that would bring with it a sense of assurance, a sense of beauty and harmony, is apparently not there.

What is it that is absent? We use words to convey ideas, but we need always to remember that the word is not the idea. The word is not whatever it is that should be conveyed, but it does, as a symbol, point to what the reality is. The word God has been used rather freely in the world, without any real understanding of what the reality was. So, many have become troubled by the word itself. I think perhaps this is rather significant. People are troubled by the word because they are so very conscious of the fact that they don't understand what it means, that they have no real awareness of the reality which is described by the word God. And there is an attempt to excuse oneself by rejecting the word. If the word is used and the individual doesn't know what it means, then he feels inferior because of that, and so he doesn't like the word. It troubles him. It draws to his attention the hole in himself. There are others, of course, who have developed some concept with respect to the meaning of this word, and they may be self-satisfied with this, and that is rather a sad state of affairs. It is far better that one should be disturbed by the word God than that one should be self-satisfied about it. It is far better that one should be honest enough to acknowledge the hole than to deny it.

The awareness of God—I am speaking here of the reality, not of the word—has been absent from the consciousness of man, and that is the hole. This absence is consequent upon man's self-centeredness. It results from his self-centeredness. In that self-centeredness he has a sense of being lost. Now of course some people build up a pretty good front around that lostness and it does not immediately appear on the surface. But as long as the reality described by the word God is absent from the experience of the person, he is lost. With all people there is, either consciously or subconsciously, a seeking for salvation, a compulsion toward the necessity of being found. The attitude underlying human self-centered function may be summarized perhaps in the words, "Save me, Lord, for I perish."

Now of course this very attitude is a self-centered one. "Save *me*, Lord, for *I* perish." The Lord to whom reference is made may relate to many things. Where there is an absence of the consciousness of God, then this hole is filled, has been filled, by what might be described, as idols. There are many such in the world. "Let the government save me." "Let the union save me." "Let technology save me." "Let my church save me." There are countless idols, both large and small, in which people put their trust, with the expectation that they will be saved by these idols. I suppose it could be said that the main aspect of sinfulness in the world might be summarized by the word "idolatry."

We might recall that our Master, when He was on earth, said something about reproving the world of sin "because they believe not on me"—"because they do not see or accept what it was that I brought, what it was that I revealed in myself, revealed for the sake of everybody else, that all might see it and accept it for themselves." Many people have tried to accept it for Jesus. They believed that. They were willing to accept it for somebody else but not for themselves. Isn't this what has occurred in the so-called Christian religion? There was a willingness to believe in another person, in Jesus. He was the revelation of God on earth. He occupied the position of the Son of God, therefore.

Many, many people have believed that, but they did not believe that in relationship to themselves, so the whole point was lost. The internal state of the individual didn't change. Each one said with respect to himself, "I will stay the way I am, although I may condescend to believe that Jesus was different. But I won't accept that difference for myself; just for Him." This was a wonderful excuse, which made people feel that they were really so good without any change whatsoever, just a belief with respect to some external thing, namely Jesus.

Now this may perhaps have caused a person to turn in the right direction, toward the reality which could begin to fill the hole in himself. But as long as he looked to something external to himself the hole remained a gaping chasm. Therefore it seemed necessary, because of this sense of emptiness, to construct what would fill the apparent need in this regard. So, many idols have been built, and people put their faith in these things. "Let the government save me. If this government doesn't succeed in saving me, then change the government." Just adjust the idol, usually more or less minor adjustments—Democrat to Republican perhaps, or vice versa. If this doesn't seem to do the job, then change the system altogether. Build a new idol, and have faith that that will get the job done. We have many political idols that are supposed to provide for man's salvation, but they're all idols. They do not speak or hear or produce anything but further chaos, disorder, conflict and destruction. So there are those who turn hopefully from political idols to religious idols. "This denomination, this school of thought, this philosophy, this belief, is going to save *me*." Or, again, to science, the god of science, the idol of science; here is the answer for sure. What marvelous technology there is in the world today, technology which takes men to the moon. And yet there are those who say,

"Well, if it takes men to the moon, why can't it deal with the mess here?" Of course, there is no answer in technology, or in any of the other idols. The answer is—God. Now, there is little recognition of the nature of this answer, and it tends to be usually a rather unsatisfactory one to most, because they have no faintest idea as to the real meaning of the word. Usually if they do have some already-established concept in this regard, that will likely stand as a barrier rather than a door, which might be opened.

It is well to acknowledge the hole, the absence, the blank. If that's what it is, then we don't know. We don't know because of the absence. The only way we can know is to let what is absent be present. If we turn to the one God (there is only one) in the attitude, "Save me, Lord, lest I perish," we have at least turned in the right direction, even though we are still self-centered. And, of course, as long as we stay self-centered we will perish. So the reason for turning to God is to emerge out of the state of self-centeredness, so that our attitude would be different. We would stop being so wrapped up in ourselves: "Save me!" Why? Are you worth saving? The self-centered person imagines that he is. Worth something to whom? Well, to himself, I suppose. But here is the very attitude which produces the trouble.

Could we put this matter of salvation a little differently? "Let God be saved in the consciousness of man." Of course God doesn't need salvation, actually; but if man is to mean anything God must be saved in the consciousness of man, because when God is entirely absent, when the hole is absolute in man, he's dead, he's perished, he's finished. And this applies to the individual, but it also applies to mankind as a whole. When man is nothing but a hole, well, there's nothing. God is something. Let God—something—be saved in the consciousness of man. If this approach is made, then it isn't a matter of "me" any more, is it? Not "Let me be saved lest I perish" but "Let God be saved in my consciousness. Let God be saved in me." This is really a very sensible approach on the basis of true self-interest, because if God isn't saved in you, then you become the evidence of the absence of God, and that's nothing. But if God is saved in you, then you become the evidence of the presence of God, and that is something.

Isn't this exactly what was revealed through Jesus, the evidence of the presence of God on earth? "Follow me," He said. "Believe in me. Let it be so for you, so that you are the evidence of the presence of God on earth. Then you are no longer plagued by this sense of emptiness. You are no longer merely the evidence of the absence of God." Of course, He is not entirely absent yet—as long as you're alive at all—but He's pretty obscure, isn't He? Why? Because of you. What other reason would there be? If God is obscure on earth it's because of us, not because of God. God is a reality, whether human beings believe in it or recognize it, accept it, or not. It makes no difference to the reality but it makes a lot of difference to people. And isn't the trouble with people?

Of course, having so little consciousness of God, we can't say definitely that God has no trouble, but we can say most definitely that man has. If we begin to see that man's trouble is simply based in the absence of his experience of God, then we begin to find the answer to a true question. Man's internal state is rotten, so his external state is rotten. Of course! This is the evidence of the presence of God, actually; the working of the Law, we might say. As you sow, so also shall you reap. This is the truth of the matter. And the truth in this sense is rising up to overwhelm man, isn't it? The waters—water is the symbol of truth—are prevailing upon the face of the earth, and man is being overwhelmed externally because of his internal state. But if the internal state is permitted to change, so that the consciousness of God comes again, then this same water, this same working of the Law, this same truth, lifts man up, so that the external world reflects the beauty and the harmony and the order of God. The flood overwhelmed everybody but those who were in the ark, but it saved the ark. Exactly the same thing is true now. The working of the Law, which causes the reflection of man's internal state in the world around him, is overwhelming man. Let that internal state change so that the consciousness of God is present again, and the reflection of that saves man. It's the same Law in each case, depending upon the state internal to the individual.

Have we reached a point, do you think, where we vividly recognize that we're not going to be saved by any of the idols? And it is not a matter of trying to find something to save ourselves, anyway. It is a matter of relinquishing self-centeredness sufficiently so that we can concern ourselves with letting God be saved in our own consciousness. How many people are interested in that, in letting the reality of being be restored in our awareness? When our internal state is the experience of that reality this will be reflected upon the screen of the world around us, just as surely as the absence of it is reflected upon the screen of the world insofar as man is concerned now. The individual is inclined to say, "Well, if I let this happen as an individual, that won't amount to very much." It won't? How do you know? If you do not know the experience itself, you simply know nothing. Of course! Because there's a hole there! Nothing is there.

The first great commandment is to love the Lord thy God with all. The first of the Ten Commandments is, "Thou shalt have no other gods before me," before this one reality. "Thou shalt not make unto thee . . ." is the second commandment—images and likenesses. "Thou shalt not attempt to fill the hole which you sense in yourself with those things which you construct in the external world around you." Now, one of the characteristics of civilized man, so called, is in the realm of his construction. Look at all the things that he has built on earth, not only material things but in the way of organizing himself; and we come again to governments and unions and churches, all kinds of things, on the grand scale, and lesser things on the individual scale, things which we trust. Imperfect, yes; we would admit that they're imperfect. But we can make improvements; they will be better after a while. We can pass some more legislation and make things better. Can anyone really believe that any more? Do you think the more legislation there is, the better things are? What would be the yardstick used for measuring?

No, the idols which men make do not answer the prayers of men. And so human beings become more and more frantic about it. They try to force their idols to answer their prayers. "Answer my prayer. Save me." But there is no voice, no answer, nothing. These are not God. They have nothing to offer. The trouble is the absence of God in the consciousness of man. And that absence produces the internal state of man, and the internal state of man reproduces itself in the world around. How absolutely ridiculous to try to change the world around into some sort of condition which would be peaceful and harmonious and delightful, a utopia, while leaving the internal state of man just the same. Let the internal state of man, of the individual, of me, be changed. That is the answer, the only one there is. Stop projecting the filth inside oneself into the world around and blaming the world around for the filth inside oneself. This is exactly what people are doing— the evidence of the absence of what one might call guts, for one thing, the fortitude, the strength of character, to accept the responsibility for oneself. Not to try to remake the world around—that can't be remade into anything but chaos on the basis of the state, the internal state, of man the way it is—but to accept the responsibility of letting one's own internal state change, never mind anybody else, so that the consciousness of God, the experience of God, is known in oneself once more. And whatever is known inside is going to come out; it's going to be reflected.

Let us be willing to save God from extinction in our consciousness. That's it. Oh, yes, in offering ourselves as a means for the salvation of God on earth—that's a switch, isn't it? "as a means for the salvation of God on earth"—we do save the world. Of course, because the world reflects the salvation of God on earth. That is the only thing that is required. The world, the reflection, will take care of itself. We don't have to push and pull it into shape. We don't know what sort of shape it should be in anyway—something different, presumably, from the way things are now, but what? "Eye hath not seen, nor ear heard, neither hath it entered into the heart of man." But it can if we're willing to let it enter in because we save God in our own experience. And that could certainly be described as eternal life, couldn't it? God's not going to duck out. Just human beings duck out. Let us be willing to save God, that thereby we may know the truth and the evidence of that truth may be reflected in the world around us. That is the experience of freedom. "And ye shall know the truth, and the truth shall make you free." None of these idols shall make you free. With God known once more to man, man is restored to his position of being the evidence of God on earth. That is the true state of man, describable by the words, "the sons and daughters of God"—the evidence of the nature and the character, the reality, the beauty, the order, the harmony, the strength, the power, of God on earth. And when

God is on earth, obviously heaven is made evident on earth. There is utopia, if you want it; but there's only one way. And that one way doesn't relate to what somebody else does but to what one does oneself, what one does about letting God be restored to one's own consciousness and experience. That is salvation.

What of the New Age?

"Now there was a day when the sons of God came to present themselves before the Lord, and Satan came also among them."

This is the day when the sons and daughters of God come to present themselves before the Lord, and Satan comes also among them. This is the day, a time of light and brightness and beauty, a fitting time, a natural time, for the sons of God to present themselves before the Lord. We gather together to this end. Why would we present ourselves before the Lord? Because we love Him, because it is our deepest desire to be near Him and to serve Him. We long to give of ourselves in serving Him on earth where we are.

And Satan is present also. "Satan" is a word used to portray the consciousness of man in his present state. I believe you are all conscious at the moment. Satan has come also amongst us. The consciousness of man is characterized by self-centeredness. This is the basis of his function and understanding in these days. These days are not much different in this regard from the days of yore. For a long time Satan has been present, dominant, in the experience of those who should be the sons and daughters of God on earth. The suggestions and the advice of the self-centered consciousness of man are followed out enthusiastically by people everywhere. This has been true of us who are here present. Satan is always one of those who is very much present in any gathering of human beings or in any single human being. His influence so completely permeates the consciousness of man that he isn't really noticed. We behave the way we do as though it were natural, as though this were the normal experience for the sons and daughters of God. Of course, most people don't even recognize the possibility of being the sons and daughters of God; Satan has complete charge; self-centeredness is absolute. It is taken so much for granted that nobody gives it any thought.

Consequent upon the state of self-centeredness there is, of course, considerable conflict between people and groups of people—inevitably so, as long as self-centeredness dominates. And while there may be a certain amount of objection to the experience of conflict and an endeavor to do away with it, apparently scarcely anyone considers that to this end self-centeredness might have to go. It appears that human beings are so wedded to the self-centered state that they can conceive of nothing else. And so Satan is certainly present amongst us. We might feel that he is not quite so dominant as he used to be, but he is present, all right.

Satan doesn't only relate to the conscious mind of man but is included in the subconscious experience. The hereditary factors out of the past are virtually all of a self-centered nature; they imbue us with self-centeredness right from the word go. And we are inclined to agree, piling self-centeredness higher and deeper. We all have degrees in this regard—Ph.D. This is the characteristic state of human beings on earth and has been for a long time.

Nowadays people are inclined to talk of the coming of a New Age, as though somehow or other some sort of a switch is being made; the magic button has been pressed, and behold! we enter the age of Aquarius, they say, as though that were going to achieve something. I was listening to Billy Graham the other evening over TV, speaking in Oakland, California. He made the statement that the end of the world is not mentioned in the Bible. It is, in the King James version. But in the newer translations it has been changed: the consummation of the age. That presumably sounds better. All this tends to cause people to imagine that they are subject to something inevitable; they really have no choice in the matter and, in any case, the evolutionary processes are working out and everything will be taken care of. Nowadays the evolutionary processes may be considered to include some sort of spiritual development as well as the usual physical changes. "Oh, we're apparently moving into a new age; everything will work out fine consequently; we don't really have to do anything about it. If things haven't been so good it wasn't really our fault; it was just the age."

Yes, there has been an age, the age of self-centeredness; not an age divinely ordained in any sense of the word, not an age inevitably imposed upon human beings so that they had to suffer under this state of affairs, not an age with respect to which God would relent one day and change the age so that we needn't continue to suffer with the troubles that have been known heretofore. The second coming of Christ, of course, has some apparent application here. According to what Mr. Graham was saying, He will show up one of these days—Jesus, that is—and set up His kingdom on earth: no more jails, no more policemen, no more cemeteries. If such a thing actually happened, I wonder how pleased people would be. I wonder how pleased those who think of themselves as Christians would be. Maybe what was set up wouldn't conform to the Baptist view, or the Catholic view, or the Methodist view, or the Episcopalian view, or the

Christian Science view, or what have you. Who would like it, do you think? And if nobody liked it, if everybody was rebellious, what sort of a state would that be? Any different from what it is now?

The government of the Lord is not absent at the moment. The laws work. In that sense everything is under control. If there is a tendency to reject and rebel against that government, then we find ourselves in trouble; we go to jail perhaps. We are in bondage, and that disturbs us even more. We want to break out. There is one thing about this jail in which we incarcerate ourselves: it is maximum security; there's no breaking out. Like many criminals in man's world we are not inclined to acknowledge the fact that we ourselves put ourselves in jail. It was always somebody else's fault. The criminal in man's world is inclined to feel that society is "agin him," but of course what he sees is his own reflection. And what we see is our own reflection. We like to impute our reflection to others or to circumstances, to things beyond our control, to the "age," or something else, which is all self-centered nonsense.

Obviously the earth is a part of the solar system, moving within the scope of the galaxy of which this solar system is a part. The galaxy itself is moving in the larger universe. There are changes in the relationships of various parts of the universe consequently. We are aware very much of the changes that relate to this earth—spring, summer, fall and winter—simply because the earth is moving in its orbit around the sun. There are undoubtedly other influences involved, the influences which produce the rise and fall of the tides, for instance, and some even more obscure to the human consciousness. So there is a changing pattern in this sense but there is nothing destructive or disruptive about such changes. They are all part of the natural design of things. They certainly do not condemn man to a state of self-centeredness; they never did. The idea that we couldn't get out of our miserable state during the age which is supposed to be coming to an end is nonsense.

Perhaps the various influences that are being brought to bear upon the earth may make it more difficult for human beings to sustain the self-centered age, but this age of self-centeredness has been deliberately sustained by human beings heretofore; they have been able successfully to do it. This is one area where man has success: he has managed to keep his self-centered state; he has managed to maintain the age characterized by self-centeredness. He could have left it behind at any time. Certainly there were many opportunities provided to enable him to do so, but no, his own attitude, his own deliberate choice, has maintained self-centeredness. To bring it a little closer to home, if a condition of self-centeredness remains in anyone here present, any of us, we have deliberately maintained it. It wasn't inevitable for any of us. We may excuse ourselves by saying, "Well, we inherited it." If someone bequeathed you a dead mouse, would you henceforth carry it around eternally in your pocket? If we have been bequeathed a state of self-centeredness, why would we continue to carry it around with us when it stinks? Just because other people do it doesn't mean that we have to do it. Just because it has become habitual in human experience doesn't mean that the habit must persist.

When we come before the Lord, do we assume the position of the sons and daughters of God? Or does Satan have free rein? Why would anyone, becoming aware of the real nature of Satan, namely self-centeredness, wish to maintain it in his own experience? If we behave in a self-centered manner, that's what we are. If we behave as the sons and daughters of God, that's what we are. Yet the attitude is so firmly held that we cannot help but behave self-centeredly at times. "I feel depressed today; therefore I must behave as a depressing person; therefore I must be self-centered!" Foolish, isn't it? The truth is present, the fact of being is present, of being the sons and daughters of God. Self-centeredness maintains our identity with the hereditary state considered to be inevitable in the world but which in fact isn't at all.

When we present ourselves before the Lord we would do so because we are sons and daughters of God. It is only because of this truth that we can present ourselves before the Lord. And we are not particularly concerned with a supposed change in the age, as though that were going to do something for us. The age changes when we change. We move into a new age when we are new people. People make the age; the age doesn't make the people. If in fact there is a movement into a new age it is because there are changes coming in people. If there are not changes coming in the people there isn't any new age. Let us not be so childishly self-centered that we look to some age of Aquarius to solve all problems. It won't. If there are problems it is because human beings have produced them. If problems in the sense of unwholesome experiences are to pass away it is because people change, because people are no longer the problems.

There are those who say that the new age is an age of groups, as though there had never been any groups on earth before. It is supposed, hereditarily speaking, that we all emerged out of the tribal systems of the past, group systems. "Now, with this new age upon us it is no longer so much the individual as the group," they say. Well, if we correlate the individual state with the self-centered state, there could properly be a change here. But one of the troubles with the world now is that there are too many groups. Because of all the groups we have the evidence of conflict. "These are going to be a new kind of group coming in this new age," they say. Self-centeredness is going to include the group more particularly now; something is going to work out that is going to be so wonderful because of groups! There is only one group that has any meaning, and that is the group which includes the whole of mankind. When the sons and daughters of God on earth come to present themselves before the Lord, no longer being subject to Satan—the old self-centered state of consciousness—then there is a true group: man as a whole. The age of that true group comes when the age of self-centeredness goes, but the going of the age of self-centeredness is not something imposed upon people, nor is the coming of the new age of the group of mankind imposed.

The world changes when human beings change. The old age goes when human beings let it go. The new age comes when they accept it. This could have happened in the past but didn't. It can happen now, and will, if there is a willingness on the part of people. And the people involved in this include the whole human race, but to be meaningful it must be seen as including you and me. The kingdom of heaven is at hand, no less so and no more so today than at any time in the past. The true experience has been available to the children of men all down through the ages. It is available now.

But there is a little word which precedes this gospel of the kingdom, a little six-letter word: r-e-p-e-n-t, repent. Oh, it is so nice to explain things on the basis of a wonderful evolutionary theory that is going to convey us automatically into the experience of the kingdom, into the experience of some utopian state, nonexistent state! The most important word on earth now, as at any other time, is that little word "repent," because until a person acknowledges the fact that he has been deliberately maintaining the self-centered state, the age characterized by self-centeredness can't pass away; neither can the age characterized by a centering in God appear. This is a deeply embedded state in human beings, summarized by the words "It's not my fault." "It's not my fault the way things are; this is the way God set it up. It's evolving." That is self-delusion. The state of affairs is the way it is because of us, because of our deliberate action; not some inevitable imposition on the part of God. He is supposed to be a loving God. Until this central point is recognized and acknowledged and accepted, so that there is repentance, nothing happens; there is no change; human beings stay self-centered. Oh, they may become "better" self-centered people, whatever that is, but the self-centeredness persists; the consciousness of man remains as it was.

An age experience isn't imposed from the outside; a change is known from the inside. While the movement in the cosmic sense, in the external sense, may bring varying influences to bear upon this earth, those influences will invariably be mistranslated as long as self-centeredness remains. And self-centeredness will remain until there is repentance. Certainly the influences that are brought to bear may seem to make it more difficult to maintain self-centeredness and survive, and this is happening. But human beings are frantically endeavoring to maintain self-centeredness and survive. Of course, in the long run it can't be done —and the run may not be too long either! In the past it has been easier to maintain self-centeredness and survive, in the collective sense. (Of course nobody ever survived in the individual sense on this basis.) So to that extent the movement of the solar system in the cosmic context does bring changing influences, that's true enough, but those changing influences do not inevitably cause men to stop being self-centered. They make it more difficult for men to be self-centered and still survive, until if they persist in self-centeredness they haven't survived.

The new age fundamentally is no different from what has been available all down through the ages. Man cannot get away with eating of the forbidden fruit. He cannot survive on that basis. He cannot survive as long as he is self-centered. That's the truth; we'd better believe it. And we'd better prove out that he does survive when he stops being self-centered. We find so many reasons, we call them, for maintaining our self-centeredness. None of them are valid. None of them have any meaning whatsoever. All of them ensure destruction. We can, if we will, behave as the sons and daughters of God, in public and in private, day and night, spring, summer, fall and winter. It is our choice.

When we come to present ourselves before the Lord in a specific sense, we come to serve Him; not to get anything to make us feel better in our self-centeredness but to serve Him as sons and daughters of God. And this is a wonderful experience if we do it. It isn't a harsh duty. If anyone is here present this morning in the Chapel who says, "Well, I wish I were somewhere else," he'd better be somewhere else! It is in fact a delight to the sons and daughters of God to serve the Lord. They don't have to be railroaded into it. We do come together to serve the Lord, to give something, to extend something, to offer something, because we have stopped being self-centered; we've stopped assuming the self-centered attitude, "Well, I need this because I have a void in me here; there is another place in me that needs to change over here; there are various things that have to work out in me, and then when all this is worked out in me I will be able to serve the Lord." Well, as long as the self-centered attitude is maintained it will be maintained; it will always be there; the empty places will be successfully preserved. But the reality, the truth, of being a son or a daughter of God is here now. It is not a matter of trying to fill up the voids that have been produced by self-centeredness—which is the effort that human beings are exerting all the time. Their self-centeredness has produced a mess, the evidence of the absence of what should be there. "So let's try and fill up this void"; in other words, try to survive while still being self-centered. It's impossible. Do you still believe the lie, "You shall not surely die. There may be a way around, you know"? There isn't.

Let us be willing to let the age of self-centeredness go, instantly. We are then in a new age, but we can't get into any new age by maintaining the old age. How beautiful to come to the point of repentance, where we take responsibility for being what we already are, instead of hiding behind this nonsensical condition of self-centeredness where we feel it's quite all right, if we feel badly or if something has upset us, to bemoan it. "Poor me!" And we excuse ourselves and say, "Well, I wouldn't be being honest if I didn't become involved in this self-pity. I behaved so badly back along the way; it was so terrible, the thing I did; therefore I must be subject to it now." And we shrink and we shrivel into nothing. That is maintaining the state of self-centeredness. "Poor me. I sinned. I am a sinner. Look at me; I'm a sinner!" Why should anyone look at you, then? Would it not be a wonderful thing if you were to say, "Look at me. I am a son, or a daughter, of God. I am exhibiting the qualities of my true nature. I stand tall and true because this is my choice. I will not maintain the age of self-centeredness but let it pass away."

"And ye shall know the truth, and the truth shall make you free." It is so. Let it be so in your constant experience.

Heaven and Earth Are One!

What a very beautiful Sunday morning this is: brilliant sunshine, vividly blue sky enfolding all, white sparkling snow, the quiet evergreen trees across the countryside. We are aware of all this by reason of our physical senses, particularly in this instance the sense of sight. But all this would be meaningless except for one thing, and that is the fact that we are alive. We have an awareness of the phenomenal world around us through our physical senses, but it is only because there is the reality of life that this phenomenal world may be appreciated, enjoyed, may have meaning. Life makes all this possible. There are those who put great store by externals. Most people tend to put their values in what is apparent in the external sense, and yet all that is nothing of itself. Life is an essential ingredient here if the phenomenal world around us is to have meaning. Where, then, is the real value? In the things of which our senses make us aware, or in the life which provides us with senses by which we may be aware?

The spirit of life relates to what has been described by the word "heaven"; the phenomenal world around us to what is described by the word "earth." Heaven and earth are one. Only man, in his foolishness, endeavors to separate them. To the extent that he is successful in this it becomes hell in his own experience.

Hell is simply the absence of the experience of heaven; it is the absence of the experience of life, in whatever degree. The experience of life as it really is, is heaven. If we exclude that experience it becomes hell. We do exclude the experience when we begin to place more value in the phenomenal world around us than in the reality of life, the quality of life. If we observe beauty around us, we are only capable of that observation because we are alive. Heaven and earth are in fact one, regardless of the widespread claim by human beings that it is mostly hell. This is an indictment upon the children of men that they should have come to this conclusion, that this should be their apparent experience. It isn't so; it isn't the truth of the matter; it is a self-made condition.

Heaven and earth are one. To be restored to a true awareness of this fact is salvation to man. The experience of this truth is available now to everyone, but most people insist that it is otherwise. There is so much that seems to be unpleasant, that seems to be wrong, that seems to be painful, unfair. There is so much apparent misery, how can it possibly be said that heaven and earth are one? As long as people insist upon this attitude, as though they imagined that this was the truth of the matter, they live in a state of self-delusion and they maintain in their own experience all the things to which they object, frantically endeavoring the while, of course, to make it otherwise. But it can't be made otherwise as long as the attitude that this is the truth of the matter exists. Here is the acceptance of a lie as though it were true. People say, "Well, just look around. Are you telling me that my experience is not hellish? It is. I know it is; I have it every day!" Well, if that's the way you want it! That's what you are claiming for yourself; that's what you are maintaining for yourself. It's not true. It's merely true from the standpoint of your own viewpoint. Fortunately your viewpoint, or the viewpoint of human beings in general, doesn't control the cosmos. It doesn't control the fact of the matter. It doesn't change anything except for the people concerned. The truth is true, regardless of the viewpoints, the attitudes, the apparent experiences, of those who deny it. If we insist upon denying the truth, we will experience what isn't true and object to it, no doubt, because it seems to be so unpleasant.

So, ignoring the area of true value, people become all "uptight" about the environmental factors, the phenomenal world around, which seems to be producing their miseries. "There is the value," they say. "Look at these miserable conditions! This is the trouble." Oh, no, it isn't. The person who accepts that viewpoint, who is involved in that experience, is the trouble. People are the trouble; not the circumstances, not the environmental world around us. As long as we are able to use these various types of external scapegoats we are trapped and the opportunity of experiencing salvation is denied to us. By whom? By the circumstances in our world? Oh, no. By our own attitude, by our own insistence upon identifying ourselves with what we conceive to be the unpleasant circumstances, rather than with the true quality of life where real value is.

It is life that gives value to all things. Our experience of life is extremely limited. We spend the days of our years squeezing it out, so that we experience less and less of it until finally we have squeezed it all out. This human activity is looked upon as being the normal state of affairs. We are born into this "vale of tears," we live a few short years, and then we die. What's the point? Most people have an inherent feeling that there must be some point to it, so they seek here and there. The vast majority think that somehow if they can grab enough out of the environment, that will give meaning to the experience; but it all seems rather futile, and it's not surprising that there is a sense of frustration and meaninglessness in people. Value is being placed where it doesn't belong, and the real quality of life remains a dream. Yet life is present to be experienced if it is valued, really, valued for itself, valued in the recognition that it is the quality of life as it really is in expression that permits the experience that heaven and earth are one.

There are those who have decided that what are sometimes called worldly things are not the answer, so they are going to seek spiritual things, assuming that because the answer has not been found in worldly things it will be found in spiritual things. If such an attitude is taken, there may be a tendency to try to withdraw from the external world in order to become more deeply involved in the spiritual world, wherever that is—an abstract experience of some kind. But this is just as much a state of delusion as being entirely involved in the external world, because heaven and earth are one. The truth of the matter is that they can't be separated. It seems that human beings are creatures of extremes, finding difficulty in obtaining a balance. We are either going to throw ourselves wholeheartedly into the material world with the expectation of gaining something or other, having fun perhaps—but it doesn't work out that way generally; it all becomes rather hollow after a while—or, on the other hand, enter into a greater experience of what is thought of as spirituality; turn away from the world, the flesh, and the devil. But the world is not going to go away; it's still there. The earth is a reality, but it's only a reality because of heaven; and heaven is a reality because of the earth. You can't tear them apart; you can't have the reality of either without the other. What a difficult problem! We can't get immersed in spirituality without drowning, and we can't get immersed in materiality without starving.

Is it not possible to find a central way? Do we have to rush from one extreme to the other in this up-and-down, seesaw existence, or may we find a firm foundation in the central way? Heaven and earth are two aspects of one thing. They are not two separate things, so that one would have to get out of the earth to get into heaven, as some have thought, and because we are in the earth, then we must have gotten out of heaven. It isn't so. If we are alive, heaven is present, available to our experience, just as the earth is present, available to our experience. I suppose, observing the beauty of the day around us, we may say that this magnificence is consequent upon the fact that the sun is shining. The radiance of the sun brings everything to life, doesn't it? We are here to appreciate it. The radiance of the sun may be seen as a symbol of the heaven aspect of the whole, and the environment around as the earth aspect of the whole. Put them together and experience that fact, that truth, because we are alive, and it is most wonderful. Heaven and earth are one!

This truth is something that has been available to the experience of people down through the ages, of course, and the memory of mankind has been jogged from time to time that it is so. We have a remarkable example of this truth portrayed through the life of Jesus. Heaven and earth are one, and He certainly exemplified this truth. "I and my Father are one," He said; but it wasn't just a matter of making statements, no matter how true. It was a matter of revealing the truth, so that there was something to back up His words when He said, "I am the way, the truth, and the life. This is it!" Perhaps He might have added, "Are you so dumb that you can't see it?" Yet it wasn't seen, and apparently it hasn't yet been seen, because Jesus has been encapsuled: in Him heaven and earth were one, nowhere else apparently! But here was a revelation of what is true, and no matter what everybody else thinks about it, it still remains true. Heaven and earth are one, and if we don't know it, what is the matter with us? We have been too busy, apparently, in placing our values where they don't belong.

One of the memory joggers that was provided by Jesus when He was on earth, to subsequent generations, was this which has become the communion service, the partaking of bread and wine. All sorts of peculiar concepts have been developed about this but, as was indicated in the record, it was a matter of bringing something to remembrance. It hasn't had this effect. In fact it has tended to obscure what should have been brought to remembrance. People have said, "This is the important thing, that we eat this bread and drink this wine; then some mystical thing happens, and that's it." But that's not at all what was indicated: "Here, do this in remembrance of me!" Of what? "Of the way, the truth, and the life, that you may recall that heaven and earth are one, and that you may begin to experience the truth of it." The partaking of the bread and wine doesn't produce the truth of it, because the truth of it is already true. It merely acts, or may act, if anyone will let it do so, as a reminder of the truth which is already true. You know, Jesus wasn't the first to offer this memory jogger. There is a story in the Old Testament about someone called Melchizedek, "King of righteousness, King of peace," who in his contact with Abraham brought forth bread and wine—symbols, memory joggers, which say in effect: Wake up from this ridiculous nightmare in which mankind has been existing as long as history goes back. That isn't very far, actually. There is some theoretical history that goes back beyond that again, but actual history, which is mostly fiction in any case, doesn't really go back very far. Did you ever read a reporter's version of a situation in which you were involved? You know very well that that description wasn't at all the way things were, at least not from your standpoint. Well, that's mostly what history is: someone's idea of the way things were. However, all that is incidental to our present consideration.

Let's get with the truth—the way, the truth, and the life—which is inseparable from the phenomenal world around us. It might be stated that the cosmos, the universe as it is in the external sense, could not exist without God. It seems more obscure to the human mind to say that God could not exist without the cosmos. The fact of the matter is that heaven and earth are one, that there are the two aspects to the one thing. We can describe these two aspects in a multitude of different ways: creator and creation, whatever. But these two are inseparable, and the earth is the evidence of heaven.

Why doesn't it seem like a heavenly place, then? Because of us, because of the way we insist upon experiencing varying degrees of the absence of heaven, the absence of life. It is said that we begin to die from the moment we are born. In other words, the way things are in the experience of human beings, the truth begins to be squeezed out of human beings from the word go. The sins of the fathers are visited upon the children, even unto the third and fourth generation. Yes, we inflict it upon subsequent generations, and then of course subsequent generations rebel against that and proceed to do exactly the same thing to their subsequent generations. We always think it is necessary to find a scapegoat. Young people blame older people; older people find plenty of scapegoats too. In any case, everybody is blaming the environment: "There's the trouble; change that around and get that set up right and we will all be happy; we will all get along together; we will all be so friendly and nice. Won't it be wonderful?" Do you think it ever happened on that basis? Of course not! How could it? because such an endeavor denies the truth that heaven and earth are already one; we don't need to make them one.

We can't make heaven appear on earth according to our concept of how it should be. In the first place, if we undertake such an endeavor we are saying that it isn't so now, therefore we have got to make it so. And that's a lie, because it is so now; and if it is so now, we can't make it so. What is necessary is that we should change our minds, change our outlook, change our attitudes, let something new appear in our own experience, not out there. If we experience heaven we find that heaven is on earth. If we try to make earth give us heaven we are left with nothing. It is our experience of heaven that makes the earth a heavenly place, and our experience of heaven has nothing to do with the circumstances around us. The circumstances around us may have something to do with our experience. If the circumstances are interpreted as being hell, why? Because hell is inside the person. That is what is being expressed by that person, and it bounces right back to him and he says, "Look, there is the trouble out there." But it isn't out there; it's in here. There is one thing I notice, in all the plans and systems and everything that people think should be instituted in the world to make it a better place: nobody ever looks at the people! It's the world out there. Of course, we may look at "them" out there, but they too are part of the environment out there. "If we could just change those people out there, then everything would be fine." Is that so!

What about us? If we see hell around us, well, I think we are identifying ourselves with the wrong person. The devil is in hell, isn't he? So, if you say, "Oh, isn't it hell!" you are saying, in effect, "I'm the devil." By the same token, if you realize it's heaven, then what are you saying? "I am God; I am the way, the truth, and the life." It seems to me this is exactly what

Jesus said, and invited others to experience. "Follow me," He said. So people go trooping along in hell! That's hardly following Him. Where is heaven? It's here! Do you think it's . . . where? On Mars maybe? If we get to Mars we can drag heaven over to the earth? Heaven and earth are one now in relationship to the earth, in relationship to Mars, in relationship to the sun, in relationship to the galaxy, in relationship to everything. Heaven and earth are one. The very fact that things work the way they work reveals it. We describe this working sometimes as "law"; we call it law; there are certain laws. Things work the way they do, regardless of how we describe it, which is an indication of the fact that heaven and earth are one. They work that way, and we can't make them work any other way. People are hopefully endeavoring to change the law of gravity somehow, without too much success so far, fortunately. This is the way things work, the way things are. Everything behaves the way it behaves. Heaven and earth are one.

If we get into a battle with it and think it should be some other way, then we are in hell. This is basically what everybody does: "Oh, we live in such a hostile environment, don't we? Everything is battering down on us, and if we don't fight back, well, we're going to be in trouble." But we are in trouble even though we fight back, because we have accepted something that isn't true. We don't live in a hostile universe. If we think so it's because we are hostile people, and we see that reflected around us. What you are in expression you see reflected around you. If you are not the true expression of the real quality of life, you see the various absences of that in your environment around you. If you are like other people you say, "Ugh, isn't that terrible! This is a miserable state. I've got to get out of it; I've got to change it; I've got to do something," ignoring the truth of the matter, namely that you yourself are the trouble, nobody else. This is so for each person: if you have troubles, you are the trouble. Most people moan about it; in fact they generally feel important because they have so many troubles. They display them all around: "Look at all my troubles, poor me!" Poor you! If a person has troubles, he is the trouble. Oh, what a shattering experience to awaken from the dream state where we feel justified in blaming everything and fail to recognize where the trouble is! Everybody does it; it's a very popular sport.

But heaven and earth are one, and we may awaken to the experience of it now. There is a wonderful theory we have these days: we're going to evolve into the perfect experience; give us another million years! Do you think we have another million years? Well, individually speaking, I don't think we have. That's not much encouragement now, in any case, is it? Who cares what's going to happen a million years from now? What's happening now is the point, and it's not a matter of evolving into something, because it already exists. It is a matter of accepting what exists. "Oh, we couldn't do that!" Particularly if we are getting on in years: "We can't change now, too late." Moses started his ministry at the age of eighty—no excuse for any of us. It is interesting to note that, in the words that have come down to us as having been spoken by Jesus, He indicated that the experience of eternal life is now, not some time in the future. You either know it now or you don't know it. The fact of the matter is that there is only one kind of life, and that is eternal, but if we separate ourselves from it in experience it seems to us to be a temporary thing. Why not accept the quality of it into expression now? and immediately we are identified with what is eternal. We don't have to wait for something. The fact that we have life now provides us with our contact point with what is eternal, but if we are all involved in the environment around us and the terrible things that are going on—this person and that person, they behave so badly and they are so unjust to me; and all the troubles there are in the world; look at the suffering that's going on; oh, isn't it terrible—if we are all involved in that, we are separating ourselves from life, and we are separating ourselves from heaven, our own experience of it. Therefore we are excluding from the earth what should be appearing here in the world by reason of our presence.

That is the blessing that we are here to offer. What's the use of complaining about all the hell there is on earth if we don't provide the heaven? When we begin to offer heaven on earth because we know heaven and earth are one now and we simply express life as it really is, instantly the experience of the world around us changes—instantly! The world that is here in this moment is the same world as will be here in the moment that we have let our own attitude change, but we will see it entirely differently. We will begin to see what it really is, not what we have thought it to be on the basis of our involvement with the phenomenal world around us. Heaven and earth are one. Earth, in that reality, is a reflection of heaven, and we begin to see it so.

Jesus said, "I am the way, the truth, and the life. Heaven and earth are one in me, in my experience; how about yours?" Most everyone says, "Oh, it couldn't be that way for me. It's all right for Jesus; He was the Son of God," etc. What was it that made Him the Son of God? The fact that He experienced heaven and earth as being one. He revealed that, and said, "Follow me!" He offered bread and wine as a reminder, that someone, sometime, somewhere, might wake up to the truth, that human beings could again begin to experience the reality of being on earth as members of a whole, as members of the body of the Son of God on earth—something in form: the earth, the bread; and something in spirit: the heaven, the wine. The flesh and the blood. The bloodstream is the life stream of God which permeates the whole cosmos. It's here on earth, available to our experience—the life stream of God, the quality of life as it really is, characterized by love and truth, present with us, waiting to find release in expression in our own living. It is seeking to come forth, that the earth may reflect it; not that the earth around us may tell us what should happen—which it does now, doesn't it? We react to something that goes on in our environment, and our environment then dictates to us the way we should behave; whereas the truth is that we should behave as life behaves, regardless of the environment; and when we do so, the environment reflects it. It reveals that heaven and earth are one. We who become conscious of these things carry the primary responsibility of letting it be so in our own experience now.

Your Significance

We are now gathered, I trust, to share some meaningful words. This should be, rightly, a very significant evening. What would make it so? I suppose you might say if I have something significant to say, that would make it a significant evening. But that isn't all there is to it, is it? because I suppose I could stand up here with nobody present in the room, just the chairs, and speak, and what occurred would not have any very great significance. The significance comes because we share something and because, I trust, we may find some basis for right agreement.

If anything creative is ever to be accomplished it requires that there be at least two people in agreement. I recall that there is mention of this principle in the Bible. Jesus Christ said, "If two of you shall agree on earth as touching any thing, it shall be done for them," etc. A basis for any right creative accomplishment rests in the fact that there are at least two people in agreement. Now it is a very, very rare thing to find two people in agreement. Two people may be in agreement with respect to some certain undertaking or other, but the agreement which is necessary for real creative fulfilment, for the achievement of some right creative purpose, is not an agreement that merely relates to some particular department of life, but it must relate to the whole of life. Two people must be in agreement all the way through. That's why I say it's something that is very, very rare.

The basis for right agreement is not established by deciding that we are going to set up a whole collection or beliefs, that we are all going to agree on these beliefs. We can say we believe some certain thing, but what is the fact of the matter? What does our living reveal as being true with respect to us? We have a lot of very sincere and earnest people who belong to churches and various schools of thought and philosophy, who subscribe to certain ideas, certain beliefs, but then all too often their lives don't reveal that this is really the fact insofar as the people themselves are concerned. It is something that is more or less of the mind and does not relate to the actual living of life. If there is to be right agreement it must relate to the living of life itself, so that the whole of the person is in agreement with the whole of the other person. Now, how would we find a basis for such agreement? We will never find it, obviously, if we all have to agree on some ideology or other, whether this relates to religion or politics or anything else. We would never find agreement on that basis, because this merely relates to a rather superficial part of the person.

We need to find a deeper base for agreement. That deeper base relates to the actual identity of the person. Now we all, presumably, think we have some sort of identity. We know the day we were born, I suppose, and the names of our parents and what name was given to us by them, and we know perhaps how much we weigh, and all these things. We have a host of statistics about ourselves, but this does not, in fact, acquaint us with who we are. These things are all related to the physical form, for one thing, the physical body: it weighs so much, it is so high, etc., good-looking, and all the rest. Or they may relate to the mind: we have had so much education, of such and such a sort. Or they may relate to the emotional realm: we have certain kinds of feelings which sometimes get out from under control. And all this is supposed to be what we are. This is what a person thinks of himself as being—all these things. This identifies him in his own eyes and in the eyes of others. But you know that anything which you can examine, anything which you can observe, anything which you can study, is not what you are. This is obviously so if you think about it. If you study your physical body, for instance, who is doing the studying? Or if you investigate the realm of the mind, if you become involved in the psychological field, who is doing the investigating? Or if you look into the emotional realm, where there is so much disturbance in human beings, who is looking into the emotional realm?

You can't examine yourself. Now this is rather contrary to the idea that many people have. All you can examine is something which is not you. It may be very closely related to you but it is not you if you can examine it, because the examiner is not the thing that is being examined. Suppose you are going to investigate yourself, and you try to get yourself over here so that you can look at yourself, well, who's going to look at it, if you get it over there? Anything which you are capable of observing and examining is not what you are. Therefore most of us are inclined to be mistaken as to our identity, because we tend to insist that we are the sort of person that appears by reason of our education, by reason of our physical appearance, by reason of our emotional state. Well, these things may all be there, but that's not what the person is, not what you are.

There is an identity, obviously, because one is capable of saying "I" or "me." There is an observer. We do a lot of observing. Perhaps some of our observing is not too accurate, but we do a lot of observing. We hear and see and feel by reason of the fact that we have a physical body to do it, and this is handy, isn't it? I don't think we would be very effective if we were here on earth just as an identity. We need this instrument, shall we call it? this body, this mind, this heart, to deal with our environment. But most people think the environment is dealing with them. There is an inclination to imagine that one is bound about by the environment. "Oh, we have such difficult circumstances, don't we, and such troublesome people who live in our environment sometimes." And all this causes us to be the way we are. And some are inclined to say, "Well, nobody ever gave me a chance. I was always bound about by all these limitations. I had a very poor childhood, oh, a terrible childhood, and this has left its mark on me." No, it didn't leave its mark on you. It may have left its mark on your physical form; it may have left its mark on your mind; it may have left its mark, emotionally speaking. But we have just seen that these things are not you. It didn't leave its mark on you at all. You are, perhaps, capable of observing the marks that have been left by these blows of fate, supposedly, but these are not what you are. It's very important that one should come to the point of recognizing this; otherwise we are going to remain subject to something to which we do not need to be subject at all: namely, the environment.

If we stop to consider the matter we may recognize, very easily, I think, that the world in which we live as human beings, which we might call the human world, was created by human beings. It didn't exist before human beings arrived on the scene. Now there is a great deal of disturbance in this world that has been created. There is a lot of turmoil and conflict, misery and suffering, tribulation of all kinds in the world, and no doubt we feel that something should be done about it to make it a better world. It's in a bad way. But it was produced by human beings, wasn't it? And we, I suppose, are included amongst that number. We played our part. Our forefathers, of course, no doubt did what they did along the way. So we have inherited a good deal, and we may complain about it. Young people nowadays—and I think in every generation, but it has become peculiarly marked in the present generation—complain about their elders. They feel that they haven't done a very good job. That may be true. I think it is true. The evidence seems to point to it. But what's the use of complaining about it? It is the way it is, and we have to deal with the thing the way it is. There are those who try very desperately to deal with the environment, this worldly environment, without too much success as a rule. And there are others who try to bow out: "Stop the world, I want to get off!" These are two extremes, perhaps. But this environment is something that has been produced by human beings; therefore we are capable of producing an environment.

Now, the one we have produced hasn't been quite the way it should be. There are apparently some glaring faults. Something needs to be done. How is it going to change? What is going to cause it to change in the right way? It is changing, anyway; everything keeps changing; but for the most part it seems to be a matter of deteriorating, or disintegrating. Even our own physical bodies tend to do that, don't they? Everything seems to disintegrate, in the end. Is this really the way it should be? One of the false views that virtually all people have, whether they have given much thought to it or not, is that they are the end result perhaps of an evolutionary process, but anyway the end result of heredity and the enviromental influences: all this has built us into what we are. But we just noticed that this isn't what we are. The things that have been built into this equipment may have been built into the equipment, all right, but it is not what we are. The equipment seems to be the end result of all this lengthy process which has come down to us from the far distant past, whether finally from an amoeba or not is a question. In any case, there has been a good deal of heredity back of us, and we have had lives of various sorts since we were born into the world—hard lives, no doubt, so many problems and difficulties, and we all have had so many things to face and deal with. Terrible! But all these things were produced by human beings. I don't think anything is gained by objecting to it or complaining about it or trying to escape it. We're here, the things are here, everything is here, and so, maybe, just maybe, we can do something about it.

If we assume that we are this equipment, that this is our identity, then we're sunk, because, after all, it is hopeless, isn't it? They tell us nowadays that if you have these traumatic experiences in early childhood and down along the way of life, then you've had it! Too bad. But there is an excuse for doing almost anything—built-in excuses for behaving any old way that we may feel like at the time, and then saying, "Oh, well, I can't help it; it's my ancestry, you know, coming out; it's my terrible childhood showing up," etc. We all have excuses for everything. What a fresh approach it would be if we decided that we didn't have any excuses for anything at all, that we have an identity which is capable of dealing with the situation just the way it is. We do not need to be identified with something which is not what we are.

When we look around in our personal environment, and when we look around in the larger world environment, we see all sorts of things that certainly are not very pleasant. We see a very great deal of tribulation, a lot of conflict, a lot of turmoil. Where did it come from? We have just noted that it was produced by human beings. If there was a time when there were no human beings on earth, this world which man has made certainly couldn't have been here. So this mess was produced by human beings. On what basis? On the basis of being identified with something which actually they are not. On the basis of being identified with this body, its mind and its emotions, so that everything is seen in the light of this. It would appear that we have a pretty good planet here; there is a lot of stuff in it. Remarkable, really, isn't it? And what a beautiful world it really is when we look at it. A beautiful world, but what a mess. What a mess!—the world that human beings have made in this beautiful world. And what do you think this world which man has made is? I think it is simply a reflection of the state that man has accepted as his own identity. In other words, if there is an acceptance of a distorted state of body and mind and heart as one's identity, then that will be reflected in the environment. While we can't look directly at ourselves, we can look at this reflection, at least. Of course, we can examine our bodies and minds and hearts, because that is not what we are, actually. But here we have an evidence of the nature of what is present in human beings reflected in the environment all around. Of course, the approach to this is, "Well, now, let's get busy. This environment isn't the way it ought to be; we want to get it straightened around so that it's all right." And what would make it all right? Or what would be all right to us? Well, presumably something that was pleasing to our own physical welfare and something that we would find mentally nice and emotionally wonderful. Unfortunately, on this basis we don't all agree, do we, as to what would be nice, as to what the right state would be.

But, in any case, how utterly futile to try to change the reflection, the state out there in the environment, without permitting any change to come in our own state of identity. If the world that man has made has been made by man, it's been made in the shape it is because of the shape that man is in. To try to fix up the world while you stay in the same shape won't work. It can't work. It's just as foolish as to say, when you're looking in the mirror in the morning, when your reflection is not quite as handsome as you are now, "Oh, that mirror is showing something terrible! I'd better get busy and change the mirror. I'd better get behind the mirror somehow and change the reflection." Well, you're not so foolish as to try that. What you do is, you change your own appearance, brush your hair, wash your face, or whatever it is, and look in the mirror again and, behold, the reflection is much better this time. Well, that's the only way the world will change—the only way.

Human beings have had a great deal of experience, over the millennia, of trying to make their world the way they want it, without doing anything about themselves. People wish to stay the way they are, with at best only a few little surface changes here and there—another suit of clothes or a different dress, perhaps a different hair-do or something, surface things; or perhaps we will change a little because we are better educated, or something else—but deep down, no change. And consequently, no change in the world, really; because before the world can change, before the reflection can change, that which is being reflected must change. There has been very earnest endeavor over the centuries, on the part of human beings, to do the impossible. And an attempt is still being made. We are going to go through all these manipulations, first of all in our own little environment, and then reaching out into the world, on the international scale—it's all the same thing—we are going to manipulate the environment into a state that we think would be pleasing to us. But it never works, because the environment constantly reflects what is present in our own nature, in our own identity.

Until the identity changes, the world won't change, at least not for the better. And this is what is happening, so we are faced with a seemingly futile situation. What are we going to do? Most people say, "You can't change human nature." Maybe. Maybe that's true, but I don't think it matters. I don't think it matters. We need to find who we really are. We need to find our true identity, and then, finding this true identity and being, consequently, identified with it, we are in position to do what needs to be done. But as long as we identify ourselves with the distorted state, with the distorted human nature, all we do is to reproduce a distorted environment all the time, and there is no possibility of anything else occurring. I would like to suggest that in our true identity as individuals we are really worth something; we really have meaning; we really have significance; we really are capable of achieving what is presently beyond our wildest dreams or imaginations. Obviously, if we are identified with the "halt and the lame"—this limited state of the human body with its mind and its emotions—as long as we are identified with that it's a hopeless outlook, because that establishes the nature of what is going to be reproduced around us. So if we don't like the things that are reproduced around us, what is it that needs to change? The things that are reproduced around us? No, not first anyway, but the thing that is producing them, and that comes much closer to home. It comes much closer to home! And it means more than a new belief, certainly more than a new hair-do. It needs something much more basic.

There seems to be an inherent fear in us all, I suppose, of the unknown. And yet, if we don't like the known, what about it? If we object to the state of the known, then we certainly need to move into the unknown. And I think that if we do undertake to move into this experience of the unknown we will find that it was not so unknown as we thought. We begin to find ourselves. We begin to find ourselves as we really are. We begin to become aware of the fact that the distorted state which we have been accepting for ourselves is not what we really are and we do not need to continue to identify ourselves with it.

This is a vital principle, because most people who are bent on self-improvement are attempting to manipulate and to change this distorted state. It is something like trying to move the furniture around in a room so as to make it a different room. Well, it may have the appearance of a different room, but it's the same room and the same furniture when all is said and done. Self-improvement, in the ordinary sense, achieves absolutely nothing because, as they say, "You can't change human nature." You may suppress some bad things so that good things appear. It's an awful strain. It's an awful strain trying to be good, and when the strain gets too much, what else is there but to be bad? To try to do the good thing by suppressing the bad thing changes nothing, really. You've still got the bad thing there lurking underneath, and when you're not looking it springs out. And anyway, what is good? What would be good, and what would be bad? I think the human judgment in this regard is rather poor. We have so many good things that have been done in the world, very good; medical progress, for instance—people kept alive when they otherwise would have died; more children, for instance, live to adulthood. And what do we have? Population explosion. That's bad! And yet what caused it was good. And we get all mixed up in these things. There are all kinds of things of this nature, where human beings think they are going to achieve something that is really worthwhile. It looks good, but after a while it turns out to be something else.

Now I am not suggesting that we should let everybody die, but what I am suggesting is that we should be concerned, individually speaking, with letting some change in our own personal identity occur, because if we accept a new identity we can willingly let the old one go. We don't have to fight against it; we don't have to struggle with the evil in it. This is what is usually thought of as the Christian view, isn't it? "Life's a battle, a terrible battle. You have to struggle so hard to be good. Of course, you can never be perfect, but you struggle so hard to be good, and it's really a fight!" Where that came from I don't quite know. I don't think it came from Jesus Christ anyway. He said, "My yoke is easy. My burden is light." He also said, "Be ye therefore perfect." So, because human beings have imagined that all this was impossible they wanted to keep their present identity, their beautiful human ego that they have built up over the years. There are some pretty fancy ones around. And everybody is concerned about their "image" nowadays. Image of what? There is this concern with fighting the bad things. We do it in our individual lives. This is magnified, and so it's done out in Vietnam, or somewhere else. We are going to clobber the bad guys. There are always good reasons for doing it, of course, and I'm not suggesting that maybe under the circumstances it may not be quite all right. But I don't think it is going to solve any problems. I believe everybody is agreed on this point. But how to get out of the jackpot—that's the question. And it's the same problem in every part of the world, because there is no way out. That's the delightful part: there's no way out, no way out at all as long as one remains the same old human being; no way out at all; we're condemned.

But we don't need to stay the same old human being. We can let our identity begin to change to something that is inherently present. It's there anyway. Maybe we have not recognized it, although everyone has touched it on occasion. But we are so intent upon the circumstances in the environment round about, we are so wrapped up in all these things. We think all this is so important, the reflection is so important—we are so mesmerized by the reflection that we want to change it around and get it to be the way we think it should be—that we ignore, completely ignore, the one thing which would permit right change to come, and that is right identity. There is a right identity present in every person; that is the person, actually. This could be described in various ways. It could be described by this statement: "The truth is, you are divine. You are right. You are perfect." But if you insist that this physical form is your identity, certainly you are not divine, and no matter what you do you can never make yourself perfect. Therefore it's quite true to say, "I can't be perfect." No, you can't, as long as you maintain that identity. But beginning to move toward a new identity you find that the old identity may be relinquished and it will pass away. It's going to pass away anyway, isn't it? Most people stay doggedly with it until the last. It goes anyway. They try to make it last a little longer. For what? Just so that there may be more distorted reflection all around? While we're still relatively alive, why not let it pass away? We might find something remarkable occurred, because, you know, your true identity is characterized by life. This false identity is characterized by death, isn't it? It's always in the process of dying, almost from the time it was born.

Because there has been no acceptance of true identity, it has been assumed that we're born into the world, we live a little while, and we die; that's all there is to it. This is the view, the usual view, the accepted view, the established view. All human beings live in this establishment. They buck it at times, of course; they don't approve of it too much; but they're caught. They don't seem to be able to get out. As long as you stay in that identity it's impossible to get out; you're identified with the thing that is going to pass away. But, being identified with what you really and divinely are in this moment, you are identified with life and you begin to find that that which is true, or characteristic of life, will be the nature of your expression through this equipment. We need the equipment still. All we are dispensing with is the wrong identity. Let it go. Let it pass away. Maybe that could be the first death. On this basis, then, beginning to discover our characterization in the nature of life, the qualities of life, so that these begin to find expression through the instrument of our bodies and minds and hearts, what do you think will happen in the environment? The environment will reflect it. The environment will have to change, not by the sweat of the brow, as human beings are constantly trying to make it change. It won't change that way. It's very tiresome, isn't it, very tiresome. And everywhere human beings look they think they have to be in a battle about something. They are in a battle with nature. Nature is going to destroy us if we don't get it under control somehow. What nonsense! Here is life expressing through nature. It's the same life that's expressing through us. It has the same character, the same quality. Let us begin to be identified with our true nature and maybe we will reveal a beauty that is comparable to the rose.

I recall that Solomon in all his glory was not arrayed like one of the lilies of the field. Why? Because the lily of the field was revealing the true nature of life at that level. But we have the capacity to reveal the true nature of life far more fully than the lily of the field if we choose to do so, if we do not insist upon maintaining this crooked, distorted, ugly human state which produces all the mess. Are we so fond of it that we wouldn't be rid of it? Of course, we've grown accustomed to it over the years. We think of ourselves as being this way and we look at someone else and say, "Oh, yes, I know him. I know the way he acts. I know the sort of person he is." Here we know all this about ourselves and about other people, but we never met each other, really; we never knew each other. We never found ourselves. We never discovered that we are characterized by the qualities and the nature, the reality, of life—something most beautiful and something most effective, something quite irresistible. Did you ever observe how irresistible life is, moving through the various forms there are in nature, for instance? Regardless of what human beings do, regardless of anything, life keeps moving. Well, are we going to align ourselves with it or are we going to be just pushed aside? We have the choice. We are capable of accepting what is now our true identity. This is life. Some say "eternal life." Well, there isn't any other kind. We accept that. We experience it now. And it's not dependent upon our environment; it's not dependent upon our own physical bodies and minds and hearts. Our physical bodies, minds and hearts are dependent upon life, are dependent upon what we are.

Then the environment is dependent upon what we are. We have it in reverse all the time. Oh, we're so beset by our environment, by the circumstances round about—"I've got to break out of this. I have no chance to be what I really am." But we have. We all have. If we choose the right identity, then we express it. And you can express it any place. You don't have to have special conditions. If you have to have special conditions, life must be pretty weak. We can express what we divinely are, and that would be perfect, wouldn't

it? We can express that in any circumstance. We don't
have to change the circumstances to suit us. We take
them as they come. And if we are permitting that
which is true of us to express through us, the circumstances will change. Simple. Much more simple than
struggling with the tremendous things that seem to be
needed in this vast environment around us. How
would we ever get it straight? It looks like a hopeless
thing, and it is, on that basis, quite hopeless. But how
quickly things can change in one's own personal individual experience, in one's own personal individual
environment, when there is the acceptance, or the beginning acceptance—it's not going to happen in a moment—the beginning acceptance of a true identity.

I am not my body, my mind, my heart. I Am. What
am I? What are you? You can't find it. You can look
where you will, you can't find it. But you can be it.
You can be it, and you know what it is as you express
it, as it comes out through you. And this is what gives
significance to the environment. Because you are present and revealing what you divinely are, because you
have accepted that identity, the moment has tremendous significance; the world is changing because of
you. All the rushing to and fro, endeavoring to make
the world be what human beings think it ought to be,
is accomplishing nothing. But the very moment you
accept true identity something begins to be accomplished. If one person does that, more is being accomplished in the world than had been accomplished by
all the other people put together. So there we are.

Let us, by reason of the acceptance of true identity,
cause our environment, our circumstances, to become
significant because we are present. The significance
appears on the basis of true identity. To the extent
that we have found some sort of an agreement in relationship to this, we will find that when we accept true
identity we are in agreement. We don't have to strug-

gle to get into agreement—"Do you agree with this? Do you agree with that?" No, we just simply *are* in agreement, because life is in agreement with itself. We are in agreement. And if there are two or more in agreement, "Behold, I make all things new." That's all it takes. Possibly it may take a period of time to reach a point of experiencing divine identity and relinquishing human identity, but once we begin to move we're on the way.

Be Thou Perfect

A particular verse in the Book of Genesis emphasizes itself to me:

"And when Abram was ninety years old and nine, the Lord appeared to Abram, and said unto him, I am the Almighty God; walk before me, and be thou perfect."

Abram was ninety-nine years old when this commandment came to him: "Walk before me, and be thou perfect." Most of us have a little way to go yet before we reach the age of ninety-nine, so we certainly could not use our advanced age as an excuse for failing to be perfect. Way back at the time of Abram (he was not yet Abraham; his name had not yet been changed) there was instruction to a human being to be perfect. We are of course reminded of the occasion when our Master said something along the same lines: "Be ye therefore perfect, even as your Father which is in heaven is perfect."

We may accept these statements as indicating what they mean. Abram was told to be perfect. There are a number of other indications in the Old Testament period of those who were perfect: "Job was a perfect and an upright man"; "Noah was perfect in his generations"; and then our Master came and said, "Be perfect." Usually it is considered that He was an example of what it means to be perfect, but He certainly did not limit it to Himself. He said, "Be perfect." Apparently this idea has not been particularly acceptable to human beings. It is such an absolute thing, is it not? It does not leave any room for excuse at all. Most people like to have a little leeway; so the idea of being perfect has been explained away by various methods, but it cannot really be explained away. It is not just a misinterpretation of the word which was originally used, or a mistranslation. The instruction to human beings is to be perfect, and if human beings are not perfect they have failed. In order to get around the sense of failure which is present in people generally—there is a deep down sense of guilt in all people, sometimes covered up pretty well, but there nevertheless—in order to get around that sense of failure to be perfect, various ways have been suggested. Usually the flat statement is made that a person cannot be perfect; no matter how hard he tries, he cannot be perfect. That of course is a true statement, because a human being trying to be perfect is incapable of being perfect, because in the first place he does not know what perfection would be. There are all kinds of ideas in that regard about what perfection would be, and they vary considerably, depending upon who you are and where you live, and what you try to believe, etc.; but if we come back to the source of perfection we begin to have a foundation for a consideration of what it would mean to be perfect.

God is perfect; human beings are not—the way they are, at least—and the commandment is, "Be ye therefore perfect." "Walk before me, and be thou perfect," is the statement which was made to Abram long, long ago, almost four thousand years ago. And using every means at his command, man has rejected the possibility of being perfect. For at least four thousand years, then, that is what he has been doing, and if he ends up in a mess—such a situation as we find in the world today—it is not particularly surprising, because he has rejected the means by which things could be different. If man were perfect, I suspect that the world would be perfect; if the world is not perfect, then it certainly is evidence that man is not perfect—and most human beings are quick to say that they are not perfect. If they make a mistake, or what seems to be a mistake, they say quickly, "You know, I'm not perfect!" as though that were reason enough for making a mistake. The question arises, then, "Why are you not perfect?"

Human beings have been trying to solve the problems of the world utilizing their methods, which they themselves admit are not perfect. So we have no solution, no possibility of solution, in fact, because the only solution which can possibly appear comes through that which is perfect. As long as it is less than perfect it is not the answer, is it? Sometimes, in the world as it now is, we have to choose between the lesser of two evils. In fact, one might say that is invariably the choice, because perfection has been rejected. So we choose the lesser of the evils, and that is the way that man imagines he should function, and that is the way he imagines he is going to find the answer to his problems. But he does not find it, does he? because the answer only comes on the basis of the answer, that which is perfect. If you have a question, an intelligent question, there is an answer to it; and the answer, if it is the right answer, is perfect. Without perfection there is no solution to man's problems, and yet he constantly denies the possibility of perfection, chiefly of course because he translates perfection according to his own idea as to what it would be; and, as we have already noted, that is a variable quantity; it is a relative thing in this world. Human concepts are notorious for not agreeing.

The Lord said, "Walk before me, and be thou perfect." He said that to Abram. Is it to be imagined that

He just said it to Abram and nobody else? I think our Master made it very plain when He was here: "Be ye therefore perfect." He did not limit it. He did not say, "Certain ones are going to be picked out, and it will be possible for them, but all the rest cannot be perfect." He never said anything of the sort. He made a blanket statement: "Be ye perfect." And that is what is required, but human beings, by their own efforts, as they themselves recognize, cannot be perfect because fundamentally they do not know what perfection would be. But God is perfect, and this fact was certainly emphasized by what our Master said: "Be ye therefore perfect, even as your Father which is in heaven is perfect." There could not be anything more perfect than that. You cannot have something more perfect, actually, can you? It is either perfect or it is not. God is perfect, and the means by which man can be perfect is God. Without God man cannot be perfect. With God man can be perfect, because man is capable of permitting God to express Himself through the human capacities.

God's expression is perfect; therefore when God expresses Himself through the capacities of any human being, that is perfect. The human being did not have to try to be perfect; he simply permitted that which was already perfect to reveal itself through him. This is the command—not just of one person here or there, not just of Jesus Christ, or Abram, or somebody else, but of every human being on the face of the earth—"Walk before me, and be thou perfect." Of course when our Master came on earth and revealed that very thing—He walked before God and was perfect—how quick human beings were to cry "Blasphemy! Look at this man saying that he is perfect, that he is the expression of the Son of God. He is just a man. Being a man, he's trying to make himself into God. Blasphemy!" The very thing that makes possible the solution to man's problems is looked upon as being blasphemy. "Oh, it was all right for Jesus Christ; He could express something wonderful on earth of God, something divine; He was the Son of God; but as for us, we cannot be perfect." Who said so? It certainly was not God. If human beings believe that they cannot be perfect they are believing a lie, because it certainly is not a statement which emanated from God. If it did not emanate from God, where did it come from? It came from the prince of liars, then; therefore it is a lie. It is a lie for human beings to imagine that they cannot be perfect. God never said that human beings could make themselves perfect, that is true; but He nevertheless said clearly enough on many occasions, "Be perfect; be perfect because I am perfect." That is God's statement, God's word; therefore if God expresses through the human capacities, there is something perfect.

How many people are too humble to acknowledge this truth? It is not humility, though, really, to say, "Oh, I couldn't let it happen through me; I am such a miserable person, such a sinner. It couldn't possibly happen through me." What a wonderful excuse! And it has been used as an excuse, and human beings have been convinced of the fact that they are sinners, which is true, but also that they must continue to be that way, as long as they live anyway. And then, after they have lived, what are they? Dead, I suspect. But, somehow or other, all this is swept under the carpet, and they are going to be perfect later on, somewhere else. Well, it is a nice idea if you can believe it. But that which is perfect is perfect now. God is perfect now, and the human being has the opportunity of providing the facilities so that that perfection can be revealed here in the world where we are; and if it were revealed, would it not be a perfect world? If all human beings were expressing perfection here on earth, revealing God, who is perfect, then everything would be perfect, would it not? We would not have to try to make things perfect. It would just be perfect. Human beings are always trying to make things over so as to be something else that they think would be better. It is not a matter of being better, or even best; it is a matter of being perfect, and that is something different. It is not a matter of improving on things; it is a matter of letting that which is already perfect find expression on earth. That will no doubt change things, but it will not improve things the way human beings want to improve things. It will be just what it is. Whether human beings like it or not is a different matter. But if perfection is expressed, perfection is here; we do not have to make it. All that is necessary is that we should be perfect. It is so simple.

Human beings think of it as a terrific struggle, even if they envision the possibility of such an idea: it is going to take ninety-nine years, for sure, to really grind out perfection; a terrific effort—blood, sweat, and tears. Do you think that will produce perfection? Do you think that is what perfection is? Is that harmonious to the expression of perfection? Do we think of God as functioning on that basis—blood, sweat, and tears? I do not think so. Perfection is entirely different; something wonderful, something perfect. God is perfect, and He said, "Walk before me, and be thou perfect." Why not let us do it, instead of just thinking about it, and talking about it, and trying to believe in something, or trying to make ourselves good, or something? The highest that human beings generally envision is something that is extremely good, but then most people do not want to be extremely good, because they figure it would not be a very satisfactory state; they would not get any fun out of life, they think—and probably they would not, according to the ideas of what it means to be good in the human sense.

But that has nothing to do with perfection, nothing to do with God—human concepts about being good.

If God is to express Himself through the human capacity—for which those capacities were created in the first place—those capacities must be in the hand of God; they must be under God's control. And what are those capacities? Well, what the human being thinks he is. It is the human being, is it not? The human being is simply a collection of capacities. There is a great deal of potential in human beings. I think there has been a recognition of this fact: that the potential that is present in people is only used very slightly. How much of the potential of your mind has been used, do you think? About ten percent? Even of the physical body? You have heard stories of the sudden strength that has appeared in certain situations through apparently puny people, like the lady who lifted the car off her son, on the spur of the moment. She did not stop to figure out that she could not do it, so she did it. So the physical capacity was there; the combination of circumstances made it possible for some of it to appear on that occasion. There have been many other examples of that sort. In other words it could be truly said, even physically speaking, that we do not know our own strength. Some people go through a lot of rigmarole to build up big muscles; and they can lift weights, and so on, which to them is important, I suppose; but is that the way to be perfect? The perfect body! Somebody is going to develop the perfect body. What would that be? An overstuffed torso—male or female? What would it be? Well, God designed man. Maybe He knows. Maybe it is just possible God knows, and maybe it is just possible man does not. Therefore what is the use of trying to be something that we do not know? What could be more futile than such an endeavor?

Let us be willing to be something which God does

know; only we cannot continue to be ourselves as human beings any more—and there is the rub. How frantically human beings want to save themselves, and one of the most popular religious ideas that has been developed is this idea of personal salvation: "Me, as a human being, I'm going to be saved! Isn't that wonderful?" Well, who would want you around as a human being? Do you get along all right all the time with everybody else, or are there occasions when it is not so good?

The human being has the opportunity of sharing something with God, and if that is shared, and God is eternal, then it seems likely that eternity might be shared; but not as a human being, not as man is in the world now, because he is not perfect. He has to be perfect to share perfection, and God is perfection. If man does not express perfection he does not share anything with God, and if he does not share anything with God, what is going to happen to him, I wonder? I do not think he is going to last very long, not even ninety-nine years. God is perfect. God is perfection. To let God express Himself through oneself as a human being is to be perfect and to share God's perfection right here and now; not waiting for some imaginary future state but experiencing the reality here and now, because the only reality you ever experience is here and now. You may have some wonderful imagination about the future, and some of it may or may not be true. Who can tell? But there is something you can experience here and now, and our Master certainly did not say, "Be ye therefore perfect fifty years from now," or after you are dead. He simply said, "Be ye therefore perfect, even as your Father which is in heaven is perfect." And the statement to Abram was, "Walk before me"—where? Here on earth of course. We have legs here; we do not know about the hereafter; some people think wings are the mode of locomotion. "Walk before me, and be thou perfect," right here on earth. God is perfect, and if we walk before God we have an indication that God is behind us in some fashion.

Now, there are a lot of people who want to have God behind them, sometimes because they simply have rejected the idea of God at all; so they put God behind them. They imagine that they have grown out of the superstitious state into the brilliance of the human intellect which knows all things, but does not know what it means to be perfect, of course. And some want God behind them to back them up in what they want to do as human beings. They want to go here or there, and do this or that: "Back me up, God, please. I think this idea is good, so certainly you should support it." Human beings are constantly trying to get God to support good human ideas, but the primary requisite for the expression of something perfect is that the means by which that expression is to appear is under the dominion of God, not that God should be under the dominion of the human being and subject to the human being's beck and call. "I want to do this; I want to do that. I want to go here; I want to go there. I want the other thing. I want your support, God, for this." The individual does not know God. What he is looking for is the genie of the lamp, the great servant who is going to serve man. Man is going to be the big "I am"—God in the background somewhere, if anywhere. But that is not the way it works. Because that is not the way it works, the world is the way it is and human beings are the way they are.

God is the great I AM; not human beings, not men and women. They could be, if they were willing—and that is the question—they could be the form on earth for God. They could be the body of God on earth. Now, there are of course ideas on that score too. But if human beings do form the body of God on earth, that which appeared through that form would be perfect.

We have a lot of claims, by this church or that religion or something else, that the members thereof compose the body of God. Where is the evidence, I would like to know? If the body of God is on earth, then it would be perfect. If it is not perfect, then there is proof positive that the body of God is not on earth. It may be in heaven somewhere but it is not on earth. The body of God cannot come on earth, cannot take form on earth, until there are those who are willing to come under the absolute dominion of God, so that they have no say whatsoever as human beings as to what should be done, when it should be done, how it should be done, or anything else—and human beings do not like that. They do not like it individually speaking; they do not like it collectively speaking. They are going to hang on to their independence, or what they call freedom, which is in fact license. Oh, they are going to exercise it with discretion, of course; they are going to be so good about it; and that is supposed to be a substitute for the perfection which God offers. But it produces all the hell there is on earth, all the suffering, all the misery—simply because human beings have not exhibited a willingness to come under God's dominion. They want to have it their own way, and if they can get God to back them up, so much the better, but if they cannot they are going to have their own way anyhow. Isn't that it?

But there is only one way that leads anywhere, there is only one pattern of function that has any future, and that is to be perfect. But a human being certainly cannot be perfect by endeavoring to be perfect himself, because as long as he is endeavoring to do anything himself he is maintaining this fat, human ego and excluding the expression of perfection from God through himself—and he cannot have it both ways. Of course the endeavor has been to have it both ways, to have his cake and eat it too. He wants to maintain his independence so that he can do as he pleases—of course he is going to figure out what is going to be good and right and all the rest, but so that he can do as he pleases—and then, because he does not like the results of this all around, it is not perfect, this horrible state of affairs that he finds himself in, he is going to develop his sciences and one thing and another so that he can get all this corrected out here. He is going to maintain his independence over here, and get the results of that independence corrected out here. He is going to make advances in the medical field and so on, so that he will be able to patch himself up, and he is going to have a good life; he is going to live longer; he is going to get more out of life, he thinks—so that he can have his cake and eat it too. He can keep his own independence and have a wonderful world. Wonderful, is it not? It could vaporize at any moment!

There is only one way which leads anywhere, and that is to be perfect; and it is absolutely impossible for anyone to experience what it means to be perfect, now or in some hereafter, without being subject to God's dominion, without losing one's vaunted independence. Those who try to keep their life, as our Master said, lose it. Of course! Those who are willing to lose it as human beings may begin to find it in the expression of the perfection of God through themselves. It is usually recognized, in what is called Christianity, that man fell because of disobedience. There are various theories as to what that disobedience was, but in principle we can certainly recognize very easily what it was: man's determination to be something all on his own, to be independent of God. That is what it is, but of course a person who becomes completely independent of God is then ready to be buried. That is the state of complete independence—death. So this endeavor to maintain independence is the endeavor to die, in fact; and human beings have been inclined to say, "Well, we'd rather have our independence and die" (which they will, for sure) "than to lose it to God and live." I personally do not think there is much of a choice. But we cannot keep our independence and serve God, and we cannot keep our independence and live. It cannot be done. It is because man is not completely independent that he has some life left for a while. It is fortunate that we are not completely independent of God, because the human being certainly would not be able to keep his physical body going, would he?—all the intricate mechanisms that are at work in the body. No, of course not. So it is obvious that, as long as life remains, man is not yet completely independent. The moment he is dead he is independent. But he may share God's freedom by becoming subject to God, by learning what it means to be obedient to God; and when he is completely obedient to God, so that he has no vestige of free choice left insofar as he himself as a human being is concerned, then he is made free; because God is free, and if God is expressing through you, you are free—you share it. That is freedom, and freedom can be experienced in no other way.

As our Master put it, "Ye shall know the truth, and the truth shall make you free." Perfection is the expression of truth; truth is a part of God's nature. You shall know God; knowing God you are free. So there is only one way of knowing God, and that is to let God express Himself through you; and when that expression comes through you, you know it, and you know God consequently. Most people are trying to know God "over there" somewhere, or up in heaven, somewhere else. They can have some bright imagination, but they cannot know God that way. It is impossible. The only way to know God is to let God come here and express Himself through you; and to the degree that He expresses Himself through you, you know

God. You may recognize God in expression through someone else but you do not *know* God that way. You know that which finds expression through you, so you cannot know God vicariously because He finds expression through someone else. That is a mistake which many of those who have called themselves Christians have made: they have thought that they could know God vicariously because of Jesus Christ. They could see something of the revelation of deity through Him, that is true. They could come to understand the principles involved and they could, if they would, be obedient to His commandment to be perfect; but unless they were actually perfect by permitting God to find expression through themselves they did not know God; they did not come to God.

So we have the privilege of sharing perfection on earth here and now, as there is a willingness to accept God's dominion personally for oneself. You cannot accept it for someone else anyhow; but you may, if you will, accept it for yourself; and fundamentally it has been man's lack of willingness in this regard that has prevented anything from happening from the standpoint of the expression of perfection on earth. It is because of this that so many of the promises which have been made by God have failed to materialize; not because God failed but because man failed—because there was a refusal to accept the dominion of God. And there is no other way. Our Master revealed that Himself. "I, of myself, can do nothing," He said. It is only the Father, God in expression through the individual capacities, that is capable of doing the perfect works; and when perfect works are done perfection results. If something that is not perfect is done, well, it is not perfect, is it? there are no perfect results. And we find things the way they are because of man's unwillingness. Regardless of all that he has said, all the beliefs he has claimed to have, fundamentally there has been this basic unwillingness. Only as there is the development of a true willingness can there be the fulfilment of this commandment, "Walk before me, and be thou perfect."

Return to Being

There is something about the matter of change which needs to be seen quite clearly. It has been very confused in human consciousness, which has tended to become hung up with the idea of evolution. I suppose the view in this regard is that things are somehow improving. The evolutionary cycles are supposed to bring an improved state, leading toward some climactic experience, I suppose. But the concept of a goal to be reached has tended to condition human thinking, so much so that some have even supposed that God Himself was evolving.

Man's experience, this unhappy and tragic interlude contained within what has been unfolding throughout the universe, must really be seen for what it is: namely, an unhappy and tragic interlude. There are those who have tried to fit it into some vast cosmic purpose. This endeavor was undertaken presumably so as to give meaning to the meaningless experience that human beings have. Instead of just recognizing that it really is a meaningless experience, there is the endeavor to try to make it have some sort of meaning. If we recognize that here is something that happened that needn't have happened, that no purpose was really served by its happening, then we begin to have a true view of the situation, so that we're not trying to make meaning out of something that in fact is meaningless. There could be no more futile endeavor.

However, because of what has taken place here on earth in the experience of mankind there certainly is the need for a cycle of outworking which would return man to the place where he belongs; so there is this seeming goal. It is in fact because man has a subconscious awareness that he is not where he belongs that he looks at everything in terms of goals. He hasn't been able quite to figure out what the goal of the universe is, though presumably he supposes there must be one. But insofar as his own affairs are concerned they all relate to this matter of goals. However, we may see that there is only one valid goal within the range of our consciousness, and that is the restoration of man to the state and the place where he belongs. Having this concept of goals in his mind he would likely say, "When I am back where I belong, what would the goal then be?" I would suggest that there isn't any goal. The idea of a goal relates to this distorted condition in man's consciousness brought about by the fact that he is out of place. Therefore there has seemed to be the necessity for a goal, or goals. Coming back into place he would discover that there is no more need for any goals.

There is a changing process in the realm of what we call creation. We may describe that as a becoming process, but becoming tends to give the idea that it is becoming better, or higher, or more perfect. All that transpires in the universe is consequent upon the being of God. God is. The true statement of being is summarized in the words, "I am that I am." This implies that I do not need to become anything. I already am.

The being of God may be said to be infinite. There is no end to it. One of the characteristics of the being of God is self-expression. God never ceases to express Himself. In view of the fact that His nature is infinite it will take eternity for Him to express Himself completely. Now, of course, the human mind boggles at the idea of eternity, so let the human mind mind its own business and allow God to mind His. The point here is that the nature of God is summarized by the words, "I am that I am." I am not more than that nor less than that. I am exactly that. And it is all-inclusive. It is all-inclusive, requiring no becoming process with respect to itself. It is. Being is being, not becoming.

The expression of being initiates what may be called the becoming processes in what we call creation. This is a changing, unfolding process, a constant creative process, because God never ceases to express Himself. But in the expression of Himself, would this mean that things become better and better? Would the expression of God be better tomorrow than it was today? It is all the expression of God. It is all the manifestation of His being. A characteristic of the being of God is perfection. God is perfect. I am that I am. That is the definition of perfection. Could the expression of God be anything else but perfect? It springs from what He is, and that expression then is perfect. The process of change is a perfect process. It is consequent upon the perfect expression of God. It can't be any better than it is, or any worse. It simply is what it is—perfect.

We may remember some words that were imputed to have come from our Master's lips: "Be ye therefore perfect, even as your Father which is in heaven is perfect." The Father who is in heaven is not becoming more perfect. What would more perfect be? One either is perfect or one isn't. It may be that the human mind doesn't know what perfection is, but it understands what the word signifies. "Be ye therefore perfect, even as your Father which is in heaven is perfect." Be perfect. Don't become perfect; be perfect. How could anything become perfect? All that is is the expression of God consequent upon the expression of the perfection of God. It is all perfect. How could it be anything else? It doesn't need to become perfect.

This is the usual concept of men with goals in mind, that somehow the unfolding processes of evolution are reaching to higher levels. Of what? Perfection? They are perfect already. Where are they going? There is this process of unfolding creative change, and it only seems necessary to have a goal because human beings are not in place, experiencing what perfection is. Because they do not have the experience of perfection in their own consciousness, then it seems as though there must be a goal that would bring them to that; and in the outworking creative cycles, of course, the purpose is to return man to the place where he belongs. But again this is always looked upon as though it were a journey, as though we had to move from here to there; but the fact of the matter is that being is perfect and we are conscious of being. Where should we go, then? Are we going to find an experience of being somewhere other than where we are?

Where we are is the only contact we have with the truth of being. If we say to ourselves, "Well, my experience of being is inadequate; I'm going to leave this one and I'm going over there somewhere and find a new one," what would you be if you ceased to be? if you left your being? Nothing, of course. Our experience of being is where we are, so we do not need to journey any place to find it. "Be ye therefore perfect, even as your Father which is in heaven is perfect." We do not need to become perfect; in fact we could not become perfect, because being is already perfect. It is a matter of experiencing what already is, and this is knowing the truth. To know the truth is to be perfect.

A person who thinks he knows the truth but does not reveal the truth through his doing certainly does not in fact know the truth.

"I am that I am." The being of God is now all that it will ever be. However, all that it is has not yet found expression. If there were some point, some goal, that we could anticipate, where the all of God finally had found expression, what would happen after that? If there is some goal toward which the whole cosmos is moving, what would happen after the goal was reached? The idea of the goal simply relates to the consciousness of man who has not known the truth; and it may seem that there is a valid goal here, because we do need to know the truth; but when we know the truth we don't need any more goal. There is the process by which we come again to the point of knowing the truth of our own identity in being. In that experience there is the consciousness of perfection. There is no further expectation of becoming anything. We are. I am. So the becoming process is simply an unfolding change that transpires by reason of the true self-expression. This is the creative expression of God. This is the Word which is with God and by which all things are created. And there is constant creation, a constant unfoldment. There are the tides of being. In this connection there are high tides and low tides. It is not all the same, not all at one level. There is movement upward and there is movement downward.

Most people have the idea that any movement downward would be retrograde. "We have got to move continually upward." In the affairs of men the idea has been (heretofore; it is being questioned now) that there must be constant expansion. In the commercial field we have to keep producing more and more goods and expand the market. But of course if you take that to its inevitable conclusion you have used everything up, and then what? It may be said that the experience of true identity in human form on earth involved a movement to a lower vibrational level. Now there's nothing wrong with that. Our present concern is to experience true identity where we are. After all, we couldn't experience it any place else, could we? It must be where we are. So we're not going anywhere to get it or to get to it. It's here. It continues to be where we are.

Some changes work out in our experience which relate to this new experience of identity. We have pictured this in terms of the opening of a door. We have heard the truth of what we are, knocking at the door. We have heard this voice extending the invitation. We hear it together this evening. Through our yielding in response the door opens, and what was behind the door insofar as what we thought ourselves to be on earth is concerned begins to come forth into the range of our present experience. There begins to be an experience of real being, so that we no longer are concerned with becoming something. Most people have dedicated their lives to becoming something. Sometimes they have a fairly clear picture of the goal but more often they aren't too sure where they're going. But they must be becoming something, they think. But as long as we have the concept of becoming we cannot experience being adequately.

It is only when we begin to relinquish the becoming process in favor of being, that we find ourselves. You can see how it is that nearly all human programs are fundamentally futile, because they are all related to attempts at becoming. Precious little consideration is given to the actual experience of being, which requires no becoming. If being already is, it isn't becoming. And if we are associating ourselves with the becoming process, we are separating ourselves from a being experience. We can't be identified with someone who is becoming and at the same time be identified with the truth of being.

Does this seem a difficult thing to comprehend? It's really very simple, but the experience of people has been so wedded to this concept of becoming, in order to reach a goal, that the simplicity of being has been overlooked. Most imagine that they have to go through some lengthy rigmarole or other in order to experience the truth of themselves, and generally people insist upon such a rigmarole simply because there is an insistence upon remaining identified with the becoming process, which is not the experience of being. There are those things which are in a becoming process, that is true. There is the creative cycle of change. But insofar as our own experience of identity is concerned, it isn't in that. That is in being. "Be ye therefore perfect, even as your Father which is in heaven is perfect," now. Our Master never said, "Become perfect," because He knew that was quite impossible. The truth of being is now, and that is the truth of what we are. To come again to the experience of this truth may be looked upon from the human standpoint as the goal. But if it is looked upon as the goal, then we must become in order to reach it; and as long as we insist upon being identified with the becoming process we can never reach it. We only find that it is the truth now when we accept the truth now.

God is what He is. God is perfect. The self-expression of God throughout eternity is the creative process. God is not becoming anything. No aspect of His being is becoming anything. There is no need to become anything in being, but the expression of that being initiates creative change in the realm of creation; and there is, then, a creative process going on in that realm. But if we identify ourselves in that realm, there we are, part of the becoming process, and we never know ourselves; we never know the truth. "I am that I am." Each individual is what he or she is in being. Changes are working out at the levels of becoming.

Now, could those changes be said to be improvements, or are they just what they are, consequent upon the expression of being? Is a stalk of corn six weeks old an improvement on a stalk of corn five weeks old, or four weeks old, or just the little shoot that's coming up through the ground shortly after the seed was planted? No, it's all perfect. The change is perfect. It's not improving. It's moving through the natural cycles of unfoldment. And it does come to a high tide, so to speak; and there we have the time of harvest. Wonderful! And so it goes with respect to all the creative processes. The idea is not to make something better than something else but to allow it to be exactly what it is. Where would the goal be, then? The only seeming goal relates to man in his distorted state of consciousness, because he feels that this isn't the way he should be. Therefore he tries to figure it out, and he says, "There must be an evolving process that is going to bring me to the state where I should be, and that would be perfect when I get there." But he never gets there, because the fact of the matter is that he is there now and doesn't know it.

So there needs to be the recognition of the unhappy and tragic interlude of fallen man on earth. This has nothing to do with the unfolding cycles of creation everywhere else. It is something that has occurred within the experience of man while the creative cycles have been moving beyond man and his experience, everywhere in the cosmos. They have been moving here too, but man has been not-so-blissfully unconscious of them, because he has dedicated himself to becoming something, having forgotten that he is something. The door opening again here—suddenly "I am." "And they were all with one accord in one place, and immediately there came a sound as of a rushing, mighty wind." Instantly the door is opened, there comes this dawning consciousness: "I am. All around me there is a becoming process, but I am." Usually it takes quite a while for a person to follow out the various patterns of rigmarole that he considers necessary in the processes of becoming something before he finally reaches the point where he ceases from all his works. "Six days shalt thou labor, and do all that thou hast to do." Six days you may go through all the rigmarole that you want; but coming to the seventh day, that's it. You have had it. You either is or you ain't.

Seemingly it is necessary to move along the way in such a manner as to cause the individual to feel that something is unfolding and he is becoming something, but in a sense it's still deception. The only value of such an experience is to reach a point where one realizes he doesn't need any more of it, and that all that is necessary is to let the door be opened. How reluctant most people are to let this happen! "Oh, I have to stay with my limitations a little longer. I have to experience this weakness a little more. I have to be subject to my troubles in order to learn another lesson." Some people spend their whole lives presumably learning lessons but they never graduate out of the state where it is necessary to learn them. God doesn't need to learn any lessons. The reality of being is. I am.

Everyone can speak those words and know something of what they mean. I am. There is something in relationship to you that is now, in this moment. It has been present all the way through in spite of all the antics through which you may have passed. There it has been right along. As the door begins to open, because there is a real yielding so that the person becomes conscious of the fact of being, he can look back and say, "Gee, I was there all the time—all the time." This is the truth for anyone but it only becomes known as it is acknowledged. That acknowledgment has been described as the opening of a door, a willingness to cease projecting the becoming process into the area where we really are. Leave the becoming process where it belongs. That is not where we belong. We belong in the experience of being. "I am." And in that experience of being there is self-expression, doing—doing, a revelation of the truth. And because of that revelation the becoming process around us intensifies, the changes come thick and fast, so that the state of the world might once again reflect the perfection of being by reason of the expression of that perfection. And there it is, because of man restored to the place where he belongs. There it is.

We are interested in seeing the whole body of mankind restored into the experience and the expression of true being. That's what we're here for. The experience of being is not really just a gradual thing. What was said about the coming of the Son of man? "For as the lightning cometh out of the east, and shineth even unto the west; so shall also the coming of the Son of man be." Most people think of dawn creeping slowly over the land. That isn't really the way it is. Such a concept relates to the idea of goals. "Well, we're gradually coming to our goal." But the lightning shines out of the east even unto the west. And lightning is sudden, isn't it? Open the door and there it is.

This is the invitation that has been extended over the ages, more particularly in recent times. Hear the knock, hear the voice, open the door. That's it. Evolution? Oh, no—no evolution involved, no evolution in being. Changes work out in the cycles of becoming but we belong in being, so that we may share with God His creative purposes here as others share with God His creative purposes throughout the whole universe. And the changing process is not to make things better but just to allow them to be what they are. The concept of one creature becoming another creature is quite unnecessary to the changing cycles of creation. Things are what they are. This is very specifically indicated, incidentally, in the story of creation in the Book of Genesis: they brought forth after their kind. As we emerge out of the concepts of men, which are merely self-centered concepts with respect to their own urge to be what they know they have never been, we begin to understand things as they are. And the universe is a beautiful place. This world is truly a beautiful place, and it is made plainly so when we and others are restored to the experience of being. And no matter where a person is, geographically speaking, he still is. There is no separation from being or in being. There is oneness, the experience of love; and there is a constant unfoldment in the world around of newness—not betterness, just newness, just the changing wonders of the Creator made manifest in the creation; not building to some sort of ultimate crescendo and then nothing more, but eternally enjoyed for what it is in the moment. And the constant striving for the goal is no longer necessary, because there isn't any goal. There's just the enjoyment of what is, just the abundant pleasure of God experienced in His creation.

To Guide You

Many people have found it not only possible but necessary to recognize and identify with the life revealed through these (and countless other) words by this author. As a new way of life was opened consequently, inevitably, for these, they began to be drawn together. A unified body of people in agreement is appearing in form on earth. There are groups of varying sizes all across the North American continent, and indeed throughout the world. This outworking of natural laws has not produced an organization in the usual sense. It is rather a living organism, the development of which might be likened to a reference contained in the Bible: a stone "cut out of the mountain without hands"; in other words, a body that has been brought forth according to a design that was not conceived by the mind of man nor built according to his planning. A new way, a proven way, is being lived by many, now and here.

This has been known by men and women of diverse hereditary, environmental, religious, economic and educational backgrounds. The particular composition of human nature did not matter. All that mattered was the unquenchable urge to find the truth in actual experience.

In connection with what has been happening in the lives of these people it became wise and necessary for practical reasons to incorporate a Society under the name Emissaries of Divine Light, with subsidiaries in many places.

Those who are interested may obtain information upon request to:

SOCIETY OF EMISSARIES

5569 N COUNTY RD 29
LOVELAND CO 80537